A history of the world's motorcycles

A history
of the world's
motorcycles

RICHARD HOUGH & L. J. K. SETRIGHT

London
GEORGE ALLEN & UNWIN LTD
Ruskin House, Museum Street

FIRST PUBLISHED IN 1966
SECOND IMPRESSION 1971
REVISED EDITION 1973

ISBN 0 04 796039 6

Printed in Great Britain in 11 *on* 12 *point Times type at the Shenval Press, London and Harlow*

Contents

	Foreword	7
1	Until 1900 Primordial chaos	9
2	1901–1915 Evolution of the fit	27
3	1916–1925 Reaching maturity	65
4	1926–1935 The classical era	103
5	1936–1949 Sophistication	137
6	1950–1972 Back into the melting pot	163
	Acknowledgments	206
	Index	207

Foreword

The motorcycle started off badly, and has suffered ever since from its self-imposed engineering limitations as well as from its despised social standing. It is one of the most pleasing paradoxes of the twentieth century that it has survived at all, to offer convenience and delight to a new generation in the 1960s, and to experience the greatest of all its revivals; for motorcycling is practised and enjoyed by more people today than ever before.

The motorcycle really began as a sort of test-bed exercise for the earliest internal combustion engine pioneers. The bicycle was ready-at-hand, cheap, light and simple. It seemed the most sensible thing in the world to secure these experimental engines to its frame. The result was an anachronistic compound, hazardous, noisy and vilely uncomfortable. But it offered the individual a new freedom; it was wanted; and it sold.

It can be argued that the motorcycle has remained an anachronism all its life, that its development has often been slow and reluctant. With the possible exception of the railways in their earliest days, it can also be argued that the motorcycle was the most anti-social form of transport. But it has also offered convenience and a special pleasure to many thousands of people in its seventy-odd years of life, from the young man of 1914 in cap, breeches and stockings, charging some rough and daunting hill on an Indian or a riotous big single Excelsior, to the booted and bone-domed youngster of 1972 threading his Honda along a winding secondary road in an extravagance of revs and banking. If to some people the motorcycle has been no more than a fleeter substitute for shoe leather and a cheaper substitute for the effete four-wheeler, to others it has been the twentieth century's hunter. For motorcycling offers a very special delight, a unique amalgam of rigour and exuberance, the paradox of detachment from the world and yet intimate engagement with it. The only comparable activity is piloting a small, nimble and open-cockpit aircraft at a low altitude—and the opportunities for this today are negligible.

So let us salute the pioneers, those who practise the ever-growing cult of the veteran and vintage motorcycle, those who have preserved this delightful machine through years of crisis and public neglect, as well as the new generation who have brought new vigour, a new renaissance, to the industry—from California east round the world to Tokyo.

Richard Hough L. J. K. Setright
March 1972

Until 1900
1 Primordial chaos

Vixere fortes ante Agamemnona
multi: sed omnes illacrimabiles
urgentur ignotique sub longa
nocte, carent quia vate sacro

When Horace wrote in his fourth book of Odes that there were great men before Agamemnon whom we would remember with respect had they not—in modern terms—lacked the services of a publicity agent, he was summarizing the dearth of early evidence that is the bane of every historian. It is common for text-books and authorities to quote the designs of the Englishman, Edward Butler, in 1884, or of the German Gottlieb Daimler in 1885, as the prototypes of the motorcycle, their choice of the one or the other depending to some extent upon their prejudices and nationality. But by more severe standards neither of these pioneers should be candidates for the honour. The idea of the bicycle is considerably older, and the idea of the heat engine dates back to the early days of the industrial revolution—indeed it may be said to have started it.

Like the first aircraft, the first motor cars antedated the petrol motor by a very long time and it is unfair to disregard the powered two-wheelers that likewise went before. After all, working models of steam-driven carriages for road locomotion had been built by Murdock and by Symington as early as the eighteenth century. At about the time when the first passenger train service had started, an English engineer named Walter Hancock built a steam-driven car which plied for hire between London and Stratford. The mere fact that we have no proper records of motorized cycles of the same period must not blind us to the possibility of their existence.

Cartoons and drawings of the period give us some clues. There was one such published in 1818 showing a two-wheeled hobby-horse or velocipede with a sort of boiler mounted on its stern and wreaths of smoke and steam conveniently hiding all other mechanical detail—or perhaps the want of it! According to the caption, this machine was invented in Germany and had been tried in Paris on April 5, 1818. Some authorities doubt whether the machine was in fact built: certainly from its appearance in the drawing it was hardly likely to prove very successful. It needed the services of no fewer than three stokers, laden with substantial baskets of what is presumably coal or coke, to raise sufficient heat for the intrepid rider to set off, and the apparent distribution of weight makes one fear for his safety once he had done so.

In the years that followed several cartoonists drew motorized cycles as well as coaches. We know that coaches existed: steam-driven carriages were running on English and French roads, and in those early days they enjoyed a surprising degree of freedom in regard to speed. A few steam cars in use sometimes maintained averages as high as 10 m.p.h. If the cartoonists were not being fanciful about the coaches, why should they be so about the cycles? In 1831, for example, Aitken drew a Regent's Park scene featuring steam-driven tricycles. Where did he get the idea for the mechanical details, if it was not from examples that he had actually seen? The artists of the day were not engineers who would know the difference between a feasible arrangement and a fanciful one.

Whatever may have happened in those earlier years, we can at least fix upon 1869 as the date of the appearance of a known motorized cycle. This, like the cartoonist's wonder of 1818, was based on that antique springless wonder the velocipede, or 'bone-shaker', which was the ancestor of all bicycles. A French one made by Michel was fitted with a single cylinder Perreaux steam engine arranged to drive the rear wheel by belt and pulleys. It had scarcely been proved to work satisfactorily before another steam-driven 'boneshaker' was built, this time by the American S. H. Roper. Fortunately, both these machines have been preserved.

The next two known examples were English, and they were tricycles. A Mr Meek of Newcastle-upon-Tyne built himself one in 1887, and Sir Thomas Parkyns designed another in 1881 that was demonstrated at the annual Stanley Cycle Show and attracted a number of orders. This could have been another industrial first for England, since it had been intended as a thoroughgoing commercial proposition; but, alas, the freedom enjoyed by the steam carriages earlier in the century had been restricted by the British Government. The Locomotives on Highways Act of 1861, supplemented by another in 1865, specified that three persons must be employed to drive a road locomotive, that a man carrying a red flag must precede the vehicle, and that the maximum speed must not exceed 4 m.p.h. It is true that the steam stage coaches were hampered in their development early in the century by the heavy tolls demanded of them, but now these speed restrictions made practically every kind of automotive activity illegal on the roads of England.

As has happened in a number of other instances, ranging from breech-loading rifles to supersonic aircraft, America developed the idea that had been pioneered elsewhere. In 1884 a Philadelphian named Copeland fitted a steam engine to a 'penny-farthing' bicycle and then went on to make a steam-driven tricycle. In fact, it is said, he made 200 of them. Historically speaking, this may be considered as something of a nine days' wonder, but there is no doubt that this was the world's first commercial production of a motor tricycle.

It is a trifle confusing that we have to consider the tricycle with the bicycle in this era. By *a priori* reasoning it might be argued that the tricycle has more in common with the conventional four-wheeled car than it has with the two-wheeler. This might in theory be true, but in practice the tricycles of the day owed their shape and constructional details to contemporary bicycle practice, and it is thus perfectly fair that we should consider them as part of this story. Tricycles figure again in the late 1880s, when two of the most distinguished names in the history of the motor vehicle, de Dion and Léon Serpollet, produced steam tricycles in 1887 and 1888. De Dion was of course Count Albert de Dion, who was born in 1856 and lived long enough (ninety years in fact) to see the revolution brought about by his pioneering work. Both he and Serpollet, who was about two years his junior and scarcely outlived the dawn of motoring, built these tricycles just as convenient test beds for their engines prior to the development of thorough-going motor cars. However, the development of the steam engine for the job was curtailed, an event of tremendous significance having occurred more than ten years earlier which was to lead to the complete eclipse of the steam engine as a motive power unit.

This event was the completion of the first practical petrol engine, devised by Dr N. A. Otto (whose name was lent to the four-stroke cycle) in 1876. To be sure, there had been internal combustion engines before then; but they were hardly practical. In 1690 the use of gunpowder had been suggested as a fuel; in 1784 the new idea for the 'explosion engine' was a piston driven by a mixture of air and spirits of turpentine vaporized on a hot surface. Ten years later such an engine was built. In 1859 E. Lenoir's engine ran on a mixture of gas and air and started off a whole generation of gas engines that became commonplace. It was three years after this that the four-stroke principle was expounded by De Rochas, to be developed by Dr Otto who patented it in 1876—which was two years after the first internal combustion engine was fitted to a four-wheeler vehicle by Marcus of Dresden.

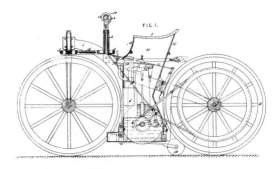

Daimler's 1885 design (**1**)

Anyway, Dr Otto was the man who really got the petrol engine going; and it so happened that he had an assistant named Gottlieb Daimler. Now Daimler was not the sort of man who could be content as somebody else's assistant. He was an extrovert who took the broad view and acted on it. In 1883 he was 49, and it was time for him to set up on his own if his ambitions were to have any hope of realization. He left the Deutz factory where Otto worked, and went to Canstatt to devote himself to the production of a small air-cooled four-stroke engine with horizontal cylinder. This was patented in 1884, and proved to be capable of turning at the then prodigious rate of 800 r.p.m. In 1885 he patented an improved vertical design that nevertheless still relied on hot-tube ignition. This system employed a tube sticking out of the combustion chamber and closed at its outer end, which was kept red-hot by a spirit burner. Into this tube mixture was forced during the compression phase of the combustion cycle; with reasonable luck, it would be ignited by the incandescent metal. A commoner kind of luck, experienced later by drivers of motors thus equipped, would see the spirit burner's flame blown out by the wind. If a motor cycle were to be dropped or capsized after a skid, the naked flame would perversely survive long enough to ignite the spilt spirit and petrol, sending the whole thing up in flames. These delights were not yet to be experienced in 1885: Daimler's engine might exist in reality, but the bicycle to carry it was only on paper.

This little Daimler engine stands out as the parent of all modern motor vehicle power plants. In 1885 Daimler patented a design for a bicycle embodying this engine and shortly afterwards he modified it, interpolating a countershaft in the drive so as to transmit the motion through a pinion meshing with an internally-toothed gear-ring on the rear wheel. It might sound barbaric to modern ears but the wheels, remember, were iron-tyred carriage-type affairs. This modified design was actually built and stands out in our history as the first petrol-engined bicycle. In November 1886 it was successfully ridden by Wilhelm Maybach, a gifted man who after assisting Daimler went on to invent the spray carburettor and thereafter to develop Mercédès motor cars at the beginning of the twentieth century.

However, if we are to include tricycles, we must return to England to examine a design that preceded Daimler's 1885 patent by one year. This came from a man of whom we know surprisingly little, despite the fact that he lived until 1940. Born in 1863, Edward Butler seems to have been a quiet man, indeed an introvert. He was married, and the evidence suggests that his wife did not share his enthusiasm for his project. It also seems likely that he had little money. Be that as it may, he had considerable ingenuity and his design for a petrol-engined tricycle displays a number of surprisingly modern features. These various ideas of his crystallized in a patent taken out in 1884: the drawings show a

Model of Daimler's 1885 machine (2)

tricycle with single stern wheel and a two-cylinder horizontal two-stroke engine, with one cylinder each side of the rear wheel driving through curved connecting rods to cranks on its spindle. It was not, however, until 1887 that he got as far as building a satisfactory version of this tricycle, by which time some of the details had changed significantly. He had apparently concluded that the four-stroke engine would be more convenient to use; but while Daimler was working with hot tube ignition, a surface carburettor, and valves of which only the exhaust was operated mechanically while the inlet was an automatic type, Butler's machine had chain-driven rotary valves and a surprisingly modern float-feed carburettor which antedated that of Maybach by five years. Another significant change in the Butler design was in the transmission. The original direct drive had been found to be quite impractical. The gearing was such that the engine was turning at a mere 100 r.p.m. when the tricycle was doing 12 m.p.h., and the paucity of power at this and even lower rates made the whole affair terribly intractable. An epicyclic reduction gear was therefore interposed, driven by curved conrods to cranks near the hub rear, these driving the rear spindle in turn by chains. At first the reduction gear was of 4:1 ratio, subsequently dropped to 6:1

The whole vehicle was extraordinarily promising and could well have been developed further; but alas, England was then no country in which to pursue such forms of inquiry. Although the need for a man to walk ahead carrying a red flag had already been dispensed with by legislation of 1878, the Emancipation Act which relieved British motorists and motorcyclists from at least some of their intolerable burdens was not to reach the statute book until 1896. In that same year Butler's tricycle, the first English motorcycle, indeed, was broken up for scrap; the man, his ideas, and his achievements faded into an undeserved obscurity.

It was far from being thus with Daimler. As soon as his motorcycle had done enough work to indicate the reliability of the engine, it was scrapped. All Daimler's efforts were concentrated upon the four-wheeled vehicle. It was for this that he had been developing his engine, and indeed the bicycle of 1885 came only after experiments with heavy three- and four-wheelers. That it should have had so brief a life is a pity, for it might have exerted a valuable influence upon other motorcycle designers in the following years. Many of its characteristics were more in accord with modern conventions than could be said of the designs of at least a score of later machines. The engine, for example, stood upright amidships, driving the rear wheel by belt. The front wheel was steered by handlebars, and both wheels were the same size. The rider sat on a saddle over the engine and had a twistgrip to work the brake.

There were other interesting designs that emerged in this period, some of them from England. Knight, for example, produced a steam tricycle in 1874 and another twenty years later. In 1892 one J. D. Roots produced what is to modern eyes the first genuine powered tricycle. This machine had a very up-to-date look about it, the two-stroke single-cylinder engine having water cooling and being mounted (upside down) behind

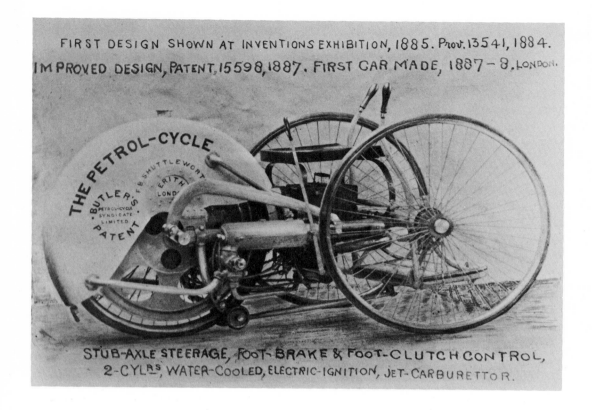

FIRST DESIGN SHOWN AT INVENTIONS EXHIBITION, 1885. Prov. 13541, 1884.
IMPROVED DESIGN, PATENT, 15598, 1887. FIRST CAR MADE, 1887-8, London.

THE PETROL-CYCLE

BUTLER'S
• B. SHUTTLEWORTH
PETROL-CYCLE
SYNDICATE
LIMITED
PATENT
ERITH
LONDON

STUB-AXLE STEERAGE, FOOT-BRAKE & FOOT-CLUTCH CONTROL,
2-CYLRS, WATER-COOLED, ELECTRIC-IGNITION, JET-CARBURETTOR.

Britain's first: Edward Butler's tricycle (3)

the rear axle which it drove through bevel and pinion gears. This engine had hot-tube ignition, and the cooling water circulated through the frame—an interesting echo from Butler's idea of a hollow rear mudguard acting as header tank for the engine-cooling water. Roots's engine as a whole is particularly interesting as an early example of the crankcase compression type; but, although the design of the tricycle as a whole predates the later commercially successful European machines, the engine must bow to Butler's machine in some respects. Having hot-tube ignition it would perhaps have no need of heated induction manifolding; but Butler's had electric ignition, and to warm the mixture there was a hot spot in the inlet tract.

About this time another name famous in the annals of motoring, this time a French one, makes its appearance on the motorcycling scene. This was a bicycle which in some ways was of most advanced design, featuring a rotary five-cylinder engine built into the rear wheel. Known as the Millet, this machine was manufactured commercially in 1894 by Darracq, but earlier examples of the machine are known.

However, the properly businesslike production and sale of motorcycles powered by internal combusion engines can be ascribed to the brothers Hildebrand of Munich, Germany. They made a start in 1899 by building a small steam engine that they meant to put into a bicycle; but they seem to have dropped the idea, and to have made a fresh start in 1892 with a small two-stroke petrol engine, followed the next year by a two-cylinder four-stroke. After so many years of summoning up the necessary courage, they

13

The beginning of the shape. 1896 Hildebrand & Wolfmuller (4)

installed this motor into a pedal cycle of the new safety type. Alas, the cycle was not strong enough; so they designed another one specially for the purpose and called it 'Motorrad' or *motorcycle*, thus originating the term.

In this form the 'bike seemed pretty sound and was therefore manufactured, by the standards of the day, in fairly large numbers both in France and in Germany. The Hildebrand brothers shared the credit for it with their assistant, Alois Wolfmuller, and the machine that they evolved between them was capable of no less than 24 m.p.h. One must remember that they had the advantage of the safety bicycle which had not been known to the earlier pioneers. Whatever the aesthetic merits of the old 'ordinary'—or 'penny-farthing' as it is more commonly and disrespectfully known—it was hardly a practical proposition for motorization. The Hildebrand and Wolfmuller was the first motorcycle to look like one. In fact it has a curious sort of resemblance to the Scotts of the 1920s with its duplex frame and water cooling.

There was also an English example of this type, a motorcycle designed by a Colonel H. C. Holden. This was almost certainly the first four-cylinder motorcycle ever, and possibly the first four-cylinder engine. The first example, patented in 1896, was an air-cooled horizontally-opposed four, but in 1899 the design was modified to incorporate water cooling. The later version produced 3 h.p. at about 420 r.p.m. and was produced for sale during the following three years. It had a reputation for being well made and certainly it must have given its riders a less harsh time than most other machines of the year, for the comparatively smooth torque delivered by the four-cylinder engine would have eliminated much of the leaping and jerking that characterized the direct-drive single-cylinder machines that were its contemporaries.

Despite all these multifarious activities, it cannot be denied that the great name of the era is that of de Dion. This Marquis, with his well-known partner Georges Bouton, formed a team that earned quite the most famous name in early motoring and motorcycling history. The men were visually an ill-assorted couple: a contemporary illustration shows them, both bowler-hatted, in their workshops; de Dion towering a clear 50 per cent taller than his partner, who was his senior by nine years.

De Dion was not the first to produce a practicable machine. He and Bouton did of course build several successful steam tricycles, but once again these were merely test beds for proposed car engines, and the firm only achieved prominence in the late 1890s when the petrol engine became predominant. To the de Dion engine France undoubtedly owed her domination of the early motorcycle industry. The first of these engines was very small, with a bore of 50 millimetres and a stroke of 60: rated at $\frac{1}{2}$ h.p., it was said to produce nearly 2. It was air-cooled and had hot-tube ignition, and more closely resembled later single-cylinder engines than anything so far.

If it was the first, it was the first of many: the de Dion firm put on the market a large number of different types and sizes of engine, nearly all of which were successful. So universal was their acceptance that by the turn of the century practically all motorcycles

14

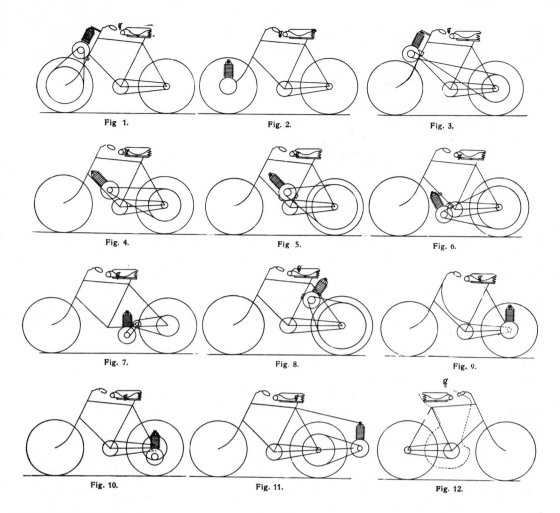

Fig 1.   Fig. 2.   Fig. 3.

Fig. 4.   Fig 5.   Fig. 6.

Fig. 7.   Fig. 8.   Fig. 9.

Fig. 10.   Fig. 11.   Fig. 12.

Where to put the engine? Turn-of-the-century variations on a theme (5)

used either the design, or parts, or complete engines. The world of commerce being what it then was, with little strict insistence on patent rights, and considerable difficulties lying in the way of those who sought to prosecute people making pirated designs, it was possible for small firms to produce the de Dion type engines and parts quite cheaply. The British were outstanding in this kind of commercial brigandry, many firms producing engines which piece for piece were perfect cribs of the original, sometimes even going so far as to use original nameplates or trademarked castings—without of course paying a penny in royalties.

Given a crude but effective engine, the would-be motorcycle manufacturers of the world loosed upon an ill-informed public an astonishingly haphazard variety of designs. Engines appeared in all the likely and unlikely places imaginable—built into the rear

1897 four-cylinder Holden (6)

wheel, or on an outrigger behind it, above it or ahead of it, clipped on to the seat stay or the front down tube, on the steering head, or over or even ahead of the front wheel. The drive was usually by twisted rawhide belt to a V-grooved pulley or rim attached to whichever of the two wheels was most fancied by the particular designer. The fact that the engine happened to be over the front wheel was no guarantee that it would be the front wheel that was driven; the serpentine courses followed by the transmission belts of some of these earlier machines bordered on the incredible, and it comes as a surprise that they worked acceptably even in the dry—we know they did not in the wet!

While most of the manufacturers hardly knew what they were doing, and scarcely any of the public knew what they were buying, the time was opportune for men whose interest was more in making money than in making motorcycles to get into the act. The middle of the 1890s marked the appearance of a number of these glib and hard-selling gentlemen, but one in particular stands out. He was an American by the name of E. J. Pennington, and he arrived in England in 1896 to market a motorcycle that was proclaimed in a welter of advertising to be the *dernier cri* of motorcycling. In fact it was nothing of the sort: we need hardly go into a list of its design features, but the absence of cooling fins from the plain steel cylinder barrels might be taken as an example. Then there was the famous 'long mingling spark' claimed by Pennington to enable the engine to run on paraffin. Another idea that got about as a result of extravagant publicity (inspired by an occasion when the prototype became momentarily airborne after hitting

1900 BMTC (7)

16

Pennington was a believer in extravagant claims and colourful advertising. This model was recommended for 'cross-country work' (**8**)

a bump) was that the machine could jump rivers! In fact only the demonstration machines were built, and it never went into production. Despite this, Pennington managed to sell his patent rights to a man named H. J. Lawson for a reputed £100,000. Lawson himself was a big-time speculator in patents, seeking to dominate the British motor and motor-cycle industry. Ultimately the trade and the press, long his sounding-board, turned on him; a patents action in 1899 brought about his downfall, and his companies collapsed.

THE PENNINGTON STURMEY MOTOR CYCLE

A more rational extension of the Pennington principle, as designed by Sturmey of *The Autocar* (**9**)

17

1898 Werner, with ¾ h.p. engine and tube ignition (**10**)

Right: A year later, and the Werner engine has doubled in output (**11**)

What could be accomplished by a 1½ h.p. Werner was demonstrated by a Mr Hubert Egerton of Weston Rectory, Norwich, England, when he accomplished the 'End-to-End' in August 1900: 'On Saturday morning the weather was fair, and I left Land's End at a quarter to five, but had not gone two miles when the sticking of an inlet valve caused a few minutes' delay. . . .' However, the great feat was accomplished, as revealed by these carefully posed 'snaps' on the rocky outcrop at Land's End, and his subsequent arrival in the north of Scotland at John o' Groat's House (12, 13)

Tricycle
and Quadricycle
Interlude

1898 Beeston two-seater (14)

For many at the turn of the century, three or four wheels were considered more stable than two, and many effective touring and racing machines of this kind were built, to reasonable standards of reliability.

(15)

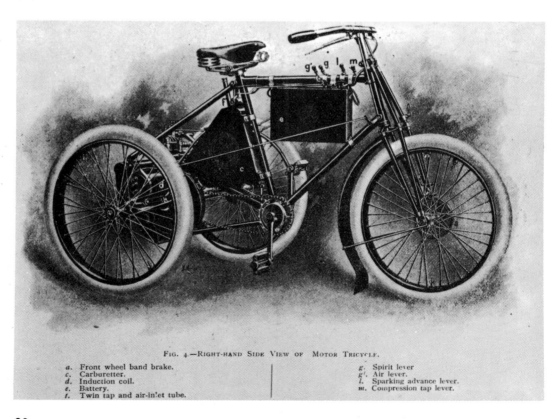

FIG. 4.—RIGHT-HAND SIDE VIEW OF MOTOR TRICYCLE.

a. Front wheel band brake.	g. Spirit lever
c. Carburetter.	g'. Air lever.
d. Induction coil.	l. Sparking advance lever.
e. Battery.	m. Compression tap lever.
f. Twin tap and air-in'et tube.	

BIRD'S-EYE VIEW OF MOTOR TRICYCLE.

Front wheel band brake.
b. Axle band brake.
c. Carburetter.
d. Induction coil.
g. Spirit lever.
g'. Air lever.

h. Silencing box.
i i'. Junction of electric wires with handle-bar
j. Switch handle.
l. Sparking advance lever.
m. Compression tap lever.

(16)

21

(17)

The Duke of Manchester, at the helm, takes a friend for a spin in his new 'quadricycle' (18)

22

The loneliness of the long-distance tricyclist. The Hon. Leopold Canning *en route* from Aberdeen to London on his 5 h.p. Century (19)

Opposite: The quadricycle and tricycle in war. The South African war saw the first use of motorized despatch riders, in this case the 2½ h.p. tricycle; and what may reasonably be described as the first armoured car. The 1899 Simms 'Motor Scout' (F. R. Simms at the helm—and trigger) carried one Maxim gun, a thousand rounds of ammunition and fuel for 120 miles (**20, 21**)

When the century was young, tricycle racing was all the rage. Here is a group of French 'racers', and *below* a 1901 Racing Phebus Aster (**22, 23**)

Examination of the motorcycles designed during this last decade of the nineteenth century suggests that with a few outstanding exceptions they were nearly all the products of ignorance or charlatanry or both. Pious and possibly misguided faith in human nature prompts the hope that this was not so, and closer examination reveals that it was not. Of course it was inevitable that a host of new ideas should be put to practical test by pioneers who could not yet have had enough theoretical knowledge to evaluate them in other ways; it was inevitable that a variety of tentative suggestions, mere probes into the possible future of the motorcycle, should be made. Some of the designs were mere suck-it-and-see redistributions of accepted components; others typified genuine technical advances. Notable was the little Gibson which had its engine built into the bottom bracket of the bicycle frame; what a pity that this did not receive more attention at the time! Also, just before the close of the century there were ladies' motorcycles built in England by Humber, by Shaw and by the Coventry Motor Company.

But ladies and motorcycles did not really go together. Indeed motorcycles could hardly be said to blend with any scene at that time. It is too early to consider their effect upon or their place in society, for they were too few in number and too dissimilar in conception. Already, however, the motorcycle seemed bound to come, for it was already proving to be cheaper to buy, more economical to run, and very often a great deal more fun than the early motor cars. Also it did not seem to break down quite so often, or at least not quite so catastrophically. For example, while the cars had an incredible amount of trouble with their tyres—the pneumatic was becoming accepted by the late 1890s—motorcycles suffered far less. True, punctures were still fairly frequent due rather to the appalling horse-battered, flint- and nail-strewn roads of the period.

There were a number of other things besides the pneumatic tyre which showed signs of fairly general adoption by the end of the century; but it will be more appropriate to consider these in our next chapter, in the light of the sudden developments which caused the motorcycle to crystallize.

The Scottish light brigade. A jaunt in 1902 by St Mary's Loch, with a mixed bag of tricycles, Locomobile, and powered dogcart (24)

1901-1915
2 Evolution of the fit

The arrival of a new century is an event that usually inspires man to new thinking, new deeds, a new type of emancipation. It may well be that the calendar helped to provide the stimulus to the development of the motorcycle, for the twentieth century began with a new irradiation of optimism in the motorcycling world. What we now call the Industrial Revolution of the nineteenth century was really a mechanical revolution, but the people alive at the turn of the century were living too close to it, perhaps, to appreciate it for what it was worth. Nevertheless they saw the twentieth century stretching before them as an age of mechanical evolution, and those who were not appalled by the thought were inspired by it. They wanted to be *of* the twentieth century, not merely *in* it. This attitude must in some degree be responsible for the sudden impetus apparent in motorcycling from the very first year of the twentieth century.

There was precious little enthusiasm for the motorcycle as the nineteenth century ended. In the Press it was stated: 'It is extremely doubtful if this class of machine will ever secure the attention of the public'; and it is not difficult to understand why. Motorcycling at that time was far from being a practical activity, far from being a sensible and predictable means of locomotion. Every trip was a special occasion, an adventure requiring a great deal of forethought and preparation, and including a number of hazards, the matter of fuel being one.

The fuel of the day was not particularly expensive, costing ninepence or a shilling a gallon in England. The carburation of the day being the imperfect kind that it was, the petrol was more volatile than would be necessary today, its specific gravity being quite low at 0·68. But it was very difficult to get: there was no question of replenishing from some convenient wayside garage or filling station. Such places simply did not exist, and along some roads one could go for scores of miles without encountering places where fuel could be bought. One of the difficulties in the distribution of fuel was that the railways were very reluctant to handle it. The special-purpose road tanker was of course unheard of then.

Fuel was not the only worry. There were questions of carbide and water for the acetylene lights as well: travel by night was quite possible, lamps adapted from those built for ordinary pedal cycles being impressed for the purpose. The oil lamp soon fell into comparative disfavour, and generally more robust acetylene types were soon developed to stand up to the greater vibration and bumping experienced on the motorcycle.

This vibration and bumping was really severe. Remember that the frames of the vehicle were precisely like those of the conventional bicycle, the 'new safety' or diamond type of which had only recently become general. There was no suspicion of any kind of springing. The front fork blades were rigid, and not infrequently they snapped. When they did so the accident was obvious, but the injury suffered by the luckless rider was sometimes serious. In addition to this hazard there was the rather doubtful adhesion of the tyres on the road. The tyres themselves, as we have said, were by now pneumatic, based on the inventions of John Boyd Dunlop in 1888, which had attained general adoption by about 1895. The wheels varied in diameter from 22 up to a more common 28 inches and the tyres they carried were of small section, never more than 2 inches across. These slender tyres, necessarily inflated to fairly high pressures to sustain the additional weight of a clumsy engine and its ancillaries, as well as that of the bicycle and rider for which they were originally devised, could not be relied upon to give anything very positive in the way of grip on the roads of the day—least of all when the absence of any springing meant that a smooth ride could only be enjoyed when both wheels were clear of the road.

And what roads they were! In the cities they were swept and watered each day, but elsewhere they were simply dirt or water-bound Macadam, rutted, potholed, uneven and filthy. They were strewn with flints, with horseshoe nails, with every kind of animal ordure, and with a mixed population of animals and citizenry, both of whom perhaps justifiably were given to fits of alarm and rage at the mere sound, let alone sight, of any mechanically propelled vehicle. When the roads were reasonably dry the passage of a motorcycle or car would be marked by huge clouds of dust, sometimes rising ten or even twenty feet into the air and hanging as a half-mile-long wake.

The basis of most machines of this time was the ordinary safety pedal cycle, now in popular use. To it was attached in a fairly haphazard manner a small four-stroke engine of de Dion type. The engine was, as we have said, mounted almost anywhere reasonable or unreasonable so long as by some means or other its motion could be communicated to one or other wheel (usually the rear wheel) by a rawhide leather belt. Attached elsewhere about the bicycle frame was an assortment of auxiliaries such as a petrol tank, a battery for the ignition system, and various control levers and linkages. The engine would be fed by a surface carburettor, the fine control of which was difficult enough without the regulation of the engine speed being made yet more precarious by the intransigent automatic inlet valve which made a wide range of engine speeds impossible. So, despite the typical little lever for adjusting the mixture of air and petrol that was usual with de Dion engines so equipped, it was necessary for continuous adjustments to be made to the ignition, advancing or retarding the spark by means of another similar little lever, usually mounted on the top tube of the bicycle frame while the cylindrical petrol tank hung beneath it.

The electrical ignition system that became standardized on de Dion Bouton engines in 1895 and general on most others by 1900 was a vast improvement on the primitive hot-tube ignition system that had earlier helped to put the petrol engine on the map. The system was basically similar to our modern coil ignition systems, comprising an induction coil energized by a small accumulator and having its primary and secondary windings so connected as to induce a high-tension current in the lead to the sparking plug through the action of a contact maker operated from a half-time engine shaft. So, in theory at least, the de Dion Bouton ignition system was reasonably practical. But unfortunately the engineering practice of the day was not sufficient to make it free from trouble. The little four-volt batteries of 20 amp-hour capacity were provided in celluloid cases; but these cases were fragile and liable to break up, or at least break down, as a result of the vibration transmitted to them through the bicycle frame. The acid within them might emerge as a fine spray that was liable to do further damage. Again, the contact-maker was fragile, erratic and difficult to adjust.

28

It would be a mistake to think that this was the first type of electric ignition system to be tried on petrol engines. The Holden machines and those produced by Hildebrand and Wolfmuller had other types of coil and battery systems; earlier still, Butler's tricycle engine was sparked by what amounted to a miniature Wimshurst machine.

It was the shortcomings of these various ignition systems that encouraged Frederick Simms, sometimes called the Father of the British Motor Industry (although with what justification is not quite clear), to look into the problem and solve it by inventing a self-generating electrical machine driven by the engine itself. Thus he produced the low-tension magneto, the prototypes of which device, which he patented in 1897, were made for him in Stuttgart by Robert Bosch. It worked. It had its limitations, but was still an improvement on what had gone before, so motor car and motorcycle engines began to embody it. However, by 1903 the high-tension magneto had made sufficient headway since the first was produced in France in 1898. Again it was the firm of Bosch who were to play the significant role, redesigning the original Boudeville magneto until it took on the form in which we have ever since known it. But it was to be 1907 before the high-tension magneto was universal, and we must revert to our motorcycle of 1901.

It would be truer to think of it as a motorized cycle. Indeed the term 'clip-on', which enjoyed a spell of popularity in the 1950s, dates back to this era when the engine was literally clipped on to the ordinary over-the-counter push-bike. It was usually clipped on at some considerable height above ground level where it had unfortunate effects on the centre of gravity and on the rider's knees or coat-skirts. Quite often it was mounted extremely far forward or aft, where it would also adversely affect the weight distribution. It became increasingly common, however, for the engine to be fitted fairly low down and as near as was practicable to the bottom bracket: it dawned more or less simultaneously upon a number of the mechanics (they would scarcely qualify for the term designers) who were building motorcycles that this was the best place.

The bottom bracket, however, had to remain free, for the pedals were still needed. The transmission systems of the day, remember, were still of the utmost simplicity, incorporating neither clutch nor multi-speed gearboxes. With only one gear and an in-flexible engine, the ability of the motorcycle to start from rest or to negotiate steep hills was very limited. Starting was either a matter of heartbreaking pedalling to get the engine turning or of a precarious run followed by an even more hazardous vault into the saddle. Hill-climbing was as hard: the idea of light pedal assistance—frequently abbreviated to L.P.A. in the literature of the day—was not as simple as it sounded. If the pedals were geared to the rear wheel in a ratio that enabled the machine to be moved reasonably at very low speeds, it would be impossible to keep them spinning fast enough to assist the engine in the speed range where it was most likely to falter on a hill—say about 10 to 15 m.p.h. So, when eventually the engine was at its last gasp, the rider was forced either to abandon the hard climb and push the machine up the hill, or else to dismount before the engine stalled and run up the hill alongside the bicycle which, relieved of his weight, might manage to keep running. In the heavy clothing necessary to protect the rider against the dust and filth of the roads, quite apart from the vagaries of the weather, such exercise induced a lather of sweat that could usually be relied upon to induce a severe chill, because of the sudden cooling breeze when the machine was started again to run down the other side of the hill or along the level.

One might say rather *if* the machine was started again. To start the engine was a matter of conjuring science, art and luck to lend their aid simultaneously. The real trouble was not so much in the carburation or ignition departments as in the poor compression of the engines. This difficulty in turn was caused by the shortcomings of the materials available in those days: there was nothing satisfactory for piston rings nor for valves.

Such terrors did the hills inspire in the motorcyclist—and indeed the motorist—of those pioneer days. There was little they could do to combat the hills, so the philosophy generally adopted was 'if you can't beat them, avoid them'. An important adjunct to every English motorcyclist's set of tools and equipment was a copy of Gall and Inglis, the little book that had been developed for the pedal-cyclists of the day, charting the gradients of all the main roads and many of the lesser passes where any but the most athletic might be daunted by the hills.

The clip-on and cycle-motor machines appeared in a variety of forms from 1897. Outstandingly successful among them all were the Minerva and the Werner. The former was manufactured in Belgium, the country in which the idea of converting a pedal cycle into a motorcycle originated. It had an engine of 211 c.c. of the usual de Dion type, with an automatic inlet valve and mechanically-operated side exhaust valve. A large number of engines of Minerva manufacture were imported into England in 1900, where they found their way into motorized cycles of many makes. Among them we may note Enfield and Quadrant and, in particular, Triumph. Nor were the English the only people to employ Minerva engines: in Germany the company who named themselves after their home, Neckarsülm, did the same. The letters NSU were extracted from this name in due course, to become the initials by which the company was ever after to be universally known.

In England, Yorkshire proved to be a county producing motorcycle manufacturers of an original turn of mind; men who were not content to do things the way everybody else was doing them. As we shall see, Alfred Scott was to be the most distinguished of these; but in 1900 the man to note was Joah Phelon, who fitted a de Dion type engine in place of the front down tube of a pedal cycle. This man Phelon later associated with another named Moore to found the P & M concern whose Panthers were famous amongst other things for having no front down tube in their frames, the sloping single-cylinder doing the job of holding the front end together.

During a later stage in motorcycle development this sloping single-cylinder layout (with or without a front down tube) was to prove exceedingly fashionable; but in 1900 it was precocious and unsuccessful. It was but one of many tentative ideas about where the engine of a motorcycle should be.

It was the brothers Werner who were to hit on the engine location that was to become generally accepted. In 1901 they produced a machine that established once and for all the new idea of having the engine incorporated in the frame rather than added to it. These two Frenchmen (for such was their nationality, though their origins were in Russia) produced a bicycle whose single-cylinder 262 c.c. engine took the place of the normal bottom bracket where the pedals were usually to be found. Special lugs there embraced the aluminium crankcase of the engine, which was now an integral part of the whole machine.

Here at last was a motorcycle which really was a motorcycle. Here was the machine which was to spark off a wave of new manufacturers, a new sport, a new means of communication, a new contribution to—or in some eyes a new threat to—society.

The success of the Werner design was tremendous. It began to be copied everywhere. Its attraction lay not merely in the integrating of engine and frame, although this in itself was a rational development, but also in the vast improvement that it made in the general handling and controllability of the motorcycle. The engine, midway between front and

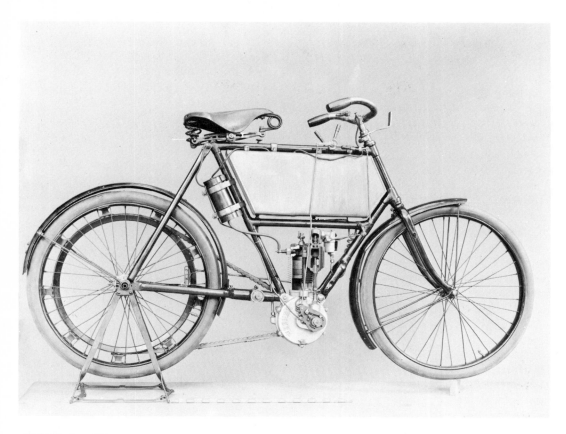

1902 Werner (**25**)

rear wheels, ensured reasonable weight distribution fore and aft; low down as it was, it reduced the height of the centre of gravity.

The new Werner had a number of other modern features: there was a spray carburettor, for example, more controllable over a wider speed range than the primitive surface types. Lubrication was by a hand pump that the rider had to remember to use every few miles: lifting and depressing it once would inject a quantity of oil into the engine crankcase, from which it would be distributed by splash and mist to the various bearing surfaces. The oil was gradually consumed as it worked up the cylinder walls past the piston rings to be burnt and exhausted. The system put a fair measure of responsibility on the rider to remember to pump and to exercise reasonable judgment in deciding when to pump. In this respect it was perhaps inferior to the drip feed system that had preceded it; but on the other hand it had the advantage that the rider could adjust the quantity of lubricating oil supplied to the engine in at least approximate proportion to the work that the engine was doing. If he was riding hard he would pump more often than he would when engaged in a leisurely potter. Riders soon learned to judge the extent of the engine's lubrication by calculating the degree of blue haze in the exhaust smoke, or to recognize the tightening up in the engine that was the prelude to complete seizure due to insufficient oiling.

Another feature of the new Werner was its rear brake. Operated by the rider's foot, it worked upon the belt rim attached to the spoke of the rear wheel, a block of fibre being forced into the rim to give the necessary friction. Such brakes were to survive for more than twenty years—and they were no better at the end of their life than they were at the beginning. If applied with any vigour when the road was wet or greasy they would lock the back wheel, promoting a sudden slide from which it was impossible to recover because the simple transmission system of the time did not allow the engine to be disconnected, so that it usually stalled. In the dry, on the other hand, the brake was feeble, partly because it lacked the necessary dimensions, and partly because of the inherent mechanical objections to supplying most of the braking effort of a bicycle *via* its rear wheel. Only recently have motorcyclists in general become sufficiently educated to appreciate the relative importance of the front brake; in 1901 simple stirrup-type front brakes were fitted, as they were to ordinary pedal bicycles, but nothing was expected of them, and indeed they were seldom used for fear of the dreaded somersault.

At any rate the Werner, if not a spectacular stopper, was at least as well endowed as any other motorcycle of its kind. In most other respects it was greatly superior, a fact that was soon demonstrated by its successes in a number of international races. In 1902, for example, it won the Paris to Vienna race under the guidance of the French rider Bucquet. There were many similar races, and in them the Werner more or less scooped the pool. Motorcycle racing had arrived: it was a primitive sort of business, but it was racing.

It may be stated as a general anthropological principle that men will always vie with each other in something or other. Thus it was natural that when two motorcyclists came together—a thing that happened not infrequently despite their small numbers—the machines should be matched against each other for speed, for acceleration or for hill climbing. Unofficial races of this sort must be as old as motorcycling itself. Organised racing took on a different shape, however, evolving in a curious way on the banked cycle tracks already built in or near some of the bigger cities, notably in England and in France. Bicycle racers had already learned the value of getting into the slipstream of another machine so as to be able to maintain the same speed without needing to expend so much energy. The advent of the motorcycle made it possible for them to ride behind a tireless and unbeatable pacer, so a number of big pacing motorcycles were built purely for this duty. They were really big: they were heavy and they carried big rear superstructures intended to act as windbreaks, close behind which the cyclist could ride free from his headwind. The motorcycles usually had de Dion or similar engines of remarkable size, lending a most brutal aspect to the whole contrivance. Built as they were without consideration of normal road-going requirements, these machines showed a fair turn of speed and it was but a short step from them to the thorough-going racing motorcycle.

Some of these things were monstrous examples of sheer primitive force and blind ignorance. Basically they featured the new Werner layout, but the tubes of the diamond frame had to be thickened and sometimes bent in order to sustain and accommodate the huge engine. Vast affairs of as much as 2 litres capacity were built. So high did the heavily-finned single-cylinder tower that there was no room for the petrol tank above it; instead, the fashionable pointed cylinder that carried fuel was stuck alongside the steering head or put out of the way somewhere else convenient. The exhaust pipe would be of drain-pipe proportions, perhaps heavily lagged with asbestos cloth here and there, and in some cases having at its end the vestigial beginnings of what we would now recognize as a megaphone diffuser. Transmission would be by a broad flat leather belt, and the whole thing would reek of improperly adapted machine-shop practice. The forks would be

solid, the tyres as big as could be obtained (which wasn't very big) and the complete machine was something that was gorgeous and terrible to behold, punishing and dangerous to ride. By 1903 the Press was inveighing against these 'racing monstrosities', particularly those from France. The not unreasonable complaint was made that these small-track racers bore so little practical resemblance to road-going machines that they were of no value either to the present as a reasonable vehicle or to the future as a source of any new knowledge.

With a variety of machines built purely for speed, not all of them being of such gargantuan proportions, the idea of properly conducted speed trials began to appeal. A typical meeting was held along the Promenade des Anglais at Nice in France. According to the *Motor Cycle* report of this event in 1903 there was a remarkable dearth of spectators. This was not altogether surprising because the event was held in the very early hours of the morning, and such spectators as did turn up were kept off at great distance for fear of accidents. The fastest time of the day by a big margin was recorded by a machine that covered the mile from a standing start in 76·95 seconds. This represents an average speed of just under 47 m.p.h., not unreasonable for a machine whose terminal velocity over the course was unlikely to be much more than 60 m.p.h. and whose acceleration was hampered by the crude transmission allowing only one fixed single gear. More than 62 m.p.h. was reached by 'the monstrosities' racing round a triangular cycle track in the Parc des Princes in Paris in the same year, but it was a more conventional British machine,

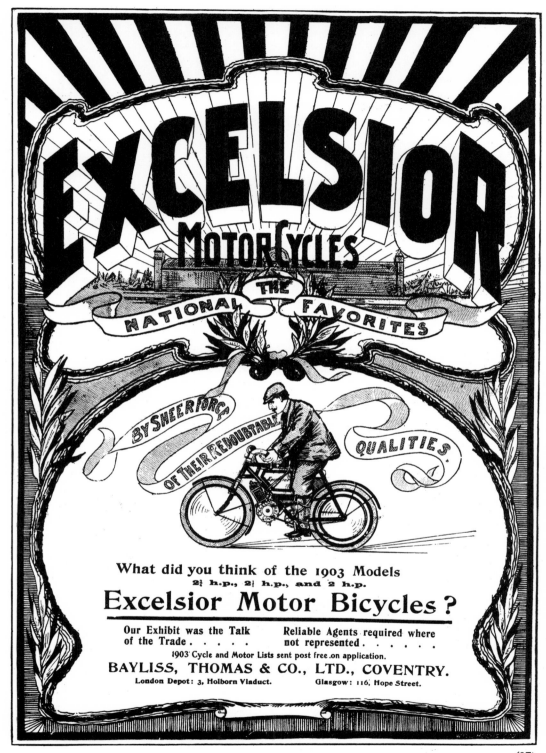

a 350 c.c. Excelsior ridden by Harry Martin, which took world records at about the same time at another cycle track, this time at Canning Town, London.

The machine was referred to not as of 350 c.c. but as of 2¾ h.p. The early days of motoring were beset by curious formulae for relating the size of an engine to the power that it could be expected to develop, formulae that were in demand by Government and sporting bodies who had their eyes respectively on taxation and sporting classification. Taking the litre as the basic unit—for was not France the home of motoring and of motorcycling?—subordinate capacity classes of one half, one third and one quarter of a litre were established, and these were recognized as being the equivalent of 3½, 2¾ and 2¼ h.p. It was not long before the 330 c.c. class grew to 350, but the non-technical men of the day were not going to have their comfortable generalities upset by a footling 20 c.c., so 2¾ h.p. remained a popular classification.

To a modern reader it may come as a surprise that, at a time when the average capacity of European and British motorcycle engines was about 300 c.c., the motorcycles being built in the USA should be smaller. Nevertheless it was so—though one must recognize the fact that as soon as the Americans were convinced of the practical or commercial uses of the motorcycle they immediately expanded their designs to give considerably more power and bulk. It was in the very early years of the twentieth century, immediately after the resounding success of the new Werner, that the motorcycling movement spread to the USA. A large number of small firms sprang into business,

Early ancestor of a great line of Indians. 1905 1¾ h.p. (28)

35

including one which under the name Thomas is popularly believed to have produced the first American motorcycle. There is no doubt, however, that, as today, the most important names in American motorcycles were Indian and Harley-Davidson. The Indian trademark was already to be seen on pedal cycles manufactured in Springfield, Massachusetts, by the Hendee Manufacturing Company. George Hendee met one Oscar Hedstrom in 1900, and the latter in the following year devised the first Indian motorcycle. It was a single-cylinder affair of $1\frac{3}{4}$ h.p., and it weighed only 98 pounds. So successful was it that in the following year it went into production, 143 being made. The next year was even better and so the little Indian went on, constantly being improved in detail until it was superseded by a $2\frac{1}{4}$ h.p. model in 1906. By that time the Indian method of engine control by twist grips rather than the conventional lever had been introduced and had seen two years of satisfactory service, echoing the twist-grip brake on the 1895 Daimler.

In Milwaukee, Wisconsin, the Harley-Davidson Company produced its first motorcycle in 1903. This, like the Indian, was a single-cylinder machine; but it was a 2 h.p. affair with a loop frame, and it stayed in production, subject to continued improvement, until 1909, when the first of the great Big Twins was introduced, a 6 h.p. V-engine of the basic type upon which Harley-Davidson has ever since relied. Perhaps it was inspired by the need to keep pace with the rapid developments from Springfield, where the little single-cylinder Indian was doubled up in 1905 to make a $3\frac{1}{2}$ h.p. twin. In subsequent years the Indian design was further modernized until both these American concerns were firmly established in the clasic V-twin field.

Similar developments, and others of equal importance, had been taking place in Europe and in England. A number of V-twins had been developed by 1905, most of them in the region of 4 to 5 h.p. and capable of being fitted quite easily and neatly into the basic Werner type of frame. This came about not merely in the quest for greater power; the single-cylinder monstrosities already mentioned showed that power could be had in abundance without the need for great mechanical complexity. However, a multiplicity of cylinders was a convenient way of getting increased flexibility and smoothness of running, and these factors were of considerable importance in any design limited by a one-speed clutchless transmission. So Minerva in Belgium, NSU in Germany, Peugeot in France, and Puch in Austria (amongst others) all evolved V-twin engines that were quickly welcomed both for solo and sidecar machines. Shortly afterwards J. A. Prestwich in England followed suit with a succession of big twins in various capacities up to 1 litre. There were also some JAP engines specially built for speedwork, including one whopper of nearly 2·7 litres. This 90-deg. twin, with cylinders of 120 mm. bore and stroke, managed a resounding 90 m.p.h. in 1908; but this was not much of an improvement on the 86 reached by a slightly smaller Peugeot V-twin at Brighton in 1905.

The 90-deg. V-engine configuration, although particularly attractive by virtue of its excellent mechanical balance (one piston reaches its peak velocity at the same time as the other is brought to a standstill at top or bottom dead centre), was not the only type of multi-cylinder engine to be developed during this period. The vertical or 360-deg. twin also saw the light of day, but only very briefly. It is interesting to reflect, now that the vertical twin has become firmly established in the modern motorcycling theme, that the great objection to the type as commonly built from 1935—a matter of imperfect balancing—was overcome in these early twins.

There are two ways of building a vertical twin. One is for the pistons to bob up and down together so that they fire at equally spaced intervals. This is all very well from the

IMPROVEMENTS

IN

1908

MINERVA

. . invade . .

Round Torpedo Brass Tank, Handle-bar Control Ignition, G. & A. Carburetter. No air lever. Detachable Footrests. Wide Mudguards. Improved Saddle. Petrol Capacity, 2¼ gallons. Oil capacity, 3 pints. Separate Carrier and Stand. No levers on tank.

PRICES.

Single-cylinder.	Two-cylinder.
2¾ h.p., £29.	4½ h.p., £39.
3½ h.p., £32.	7-8 h.p., £45

Magneto Ignition, £5 extra.

Spring Forks, £2 10s. extra.

EASY PAYMENTS ARRANGED.

1908 Booklet post free on request.

MINERVA MOTORS, Ltd.

40, HOLBORN VIADUCT, LONDON, E.C.

Minerva Goods and Repairs, Ltd., 15-17, Charlotte Street, W.

AGENTS.

ACCRINGTON—
Athletic Supply Association.
BIRMINGHAM—
Heath & Co., 49, John Bright Street.
BRIGHTON—
W. Cowderoy, 7, Gloucester Road.
BRISTOL—
The Olympia Motor and Engineering Works, St. James' Square.
BOLTON—
J. H. Green, 186, Derby Street.
BURNLEY—
J. Hebden, Waterloo Road.
DONCASTER—
W. E. Clarke & Co., Station Road.
HALIFAX—
Harry Maude, 2, Lilly Lane.
HULL—
E. S. Annison, 33-34, Witham Street.
LIVERPOOL—
Gormlys, Ltd., Berry Street.
MANCHESTER—
Cookson & Bros., 511, Chester Road, Old Trafford.
MIDDLESBROUGH—
Upton's Stores, 6, Newport Crescent.

AGENTS.

NOTTINGHAM—
E. G. Young & Co., Bentinck Motor Works, Trent Bridge.
NEWCASTLE-ON-TYNE—
Eldon Electric Co., 61, High Bridge.
PETERBOROUGH—
Heightons Depots, Ltd., 51, Westgate.
SOUTHWELL—
J. Mather & Co., King Street.
STOCKPORT (near)—
J. Garlick Looker & Co., Portland Grove, Heaton Chapel.
WORCESTER—
Barker's Garage, Lowesmoor Place.
CARDIFF—
Robert Bevan, 31, Castle Street.
GLASGOW—
Jas. Gibbon & Sons, 98, West Nile Street.
BELFAST—
J. B. Ferguson, Ltd., Little Donegall Street.
DUBLIN—
H. S. Huet, 5, South Anne Street.

A.J.W.

(29)

point of view of even torque delivery, but from the point of view of mechanical balance such a twin is merely tantamount to two single-cylinder engines going 'bump!' together; and of course the single-cylinder engine is incapable of proper balancing. In other words, the smooth power delivery was obtained at the sacrifice of inevitable vibration. The other way to build a vertical twin is to have the crank pins spaced 180 deg. apart: this gives a far better mechanical balance—indeed the primary balance is perfect—but the power impulses are no longer evenly spaced, occurring instead at intervals 180 deg. and 540 deg. Later versions of the 1905 5 h.p. Berclay twin-cylinder engine, for example, were built in this way.

As any devotee of Douglas or BMW machines will hasten to tell you, the simple solution to the problems of balance and equal firing impulses in two-cylinder engines is to arrange the cylinders so that they are horizontally opposed. This layout ensures smooth torque, perfect primary balance and (provided that the two cylinders are not unduly offset relative to each other to accommodate side-by-side connecting rods) almost perfect secondary balance with only a slight rocking couple. Such an engine is particularly attractive for installation in a motorcycle: if arranged so that the cylinders are in the transverse plane, they project into the airstream and are guaranteed a sufficiency of cooling air, while if they are disposed fore and aft to simplify the transmission they can still be arranged low down so as to give the bicycle a low centre of gravity and so endow it with basically good handling potential. The Barry was one of the first such engines to be put into a motorcycle in 1904, but it was a flash in the pan. Not until 1906 did Douglas Motors Ltd. of Bristol establish their flat twin, a 2¼ h.p. engine with a big flywheel outside the crankcase driving through a primary chain to a countershaft whence a belt drove the rear wheel. In 1907 Douglas went a stage further to the first of their famous 2¾ h.p. models, this time with direct belt drive. The flat twin has been a traditional Douglas characteristic ever since, right up to the ill-fated Dragonfly which was the last motorcycle the Kingswood firm ever built.

There were 4-cylinder engines in this period as well. A Nottingham man named Binks produced a 5 h.p. in-line four in 1903, though it did not go into production. By contrast the 363 c.c. FN of 1905, complete with shaft and bevel-gear drive to the rear wheel, and internal expanding rear brake and telescopic front forks, was an overwhelming success and remained in production in successively improved forms until 1925. But the FN engine, despite its multiplicity of cylinders, was not notably powerful, nor the bicycle particularly fast. The whole object of having four cylinders was to achieve smooth running and a greater measure of flexibility, for the machine was still hampered by its single-speed transmission. Indeed, pedalling gear was still fitted.

With the century five or six years old and the motorcycle itself just attaining its majority, improvements began to come thick and fast. It was not before time, for the market to which motorcycles were intended to appeal embraced men of a quite different type from the pioneer riders. Those hardy and obsessively enthusiastic fellows who put the new sport on its feet were now something of a minority; the men who were now buying motorcycles looked to them not merely for sport but also for transport. The new owner would entertain no romantic notions about his machine, and usually had no mechanical knowledge whatever. It was therefore necessary for the motorcycle to advance to a greater level of reliability and of versatility.

And so indeed it did. In the years from 1905 until 1916 practically every modern design feature made its appearance. There were sprung front forks, for example, on the FN of 1905 and the Douglas of 1908. The rather awkward tank-top control levers and

The arrangement of cylinders led to as many experiments and variations as the location of the engine itself. Here are two examples of early multi-cylinder motorcycles, the Pierce Arrow from America, and the Motosacoche from Switzerland, a highly speculative radial (30, 31)

rigid linkages of the early machines were supplanted by flexible Bowden cables which enabled the air, mixture and ignition levers to be mounted on the handlebars so that the rider could operate them without moving his hands. The Bosch high-tension magneto and other similar types became firmly established by 1907 on practically all motorcycles. By 1903 the old round twisted rawhide driving belt was replaced by a leather one of V-section, and shortly afterwards by the new and longer-lasting combination of rubber-and-canvas belting. A number of French and American motorcycles featured chain drive instead of belts, more positive (particularly in the wet) but also far more harsh. Tyres grew better and also fatter, the largest motorcycles commonly running on sections of $2\frac{3}{8}$ or $2\frac{1}{2}$ inches, and Indians on 3 inch tyres. Indians were also notable for having one of the best spring frames of the period, the rear forks being suspended by quarter-elliptic leaf springs. Many other firms devised various types of articulation for the rear part of the frame as well.

Motorcycles even began to be fitted with instruments, notably speedometers of various makes. Of all these the Bonniksen was the outstanding one, being virtually a collector's piece; it embodied an elaborate clockwork escapement which justified the 'Isochronous' label of the Bonniksen by alternately prodding each of a pair of pointers around the dial to indicate the speed every five seconds, while minor dials scattered about the face recorded distances covered. It was all very endearing, but hardly as practical as the simple centrifugal affairs that grew into the instruments we have today.

The electrical system grew more extensive in this period too. Many bicycles still enjoyed nothing better than acetylene lamps, although the production in 1912 of the dissolved acetylene system, with small steel cylinders holding the gas all ready for piping to the lamp jets, relieved the rider of the tricky business of adjusting water jets and cleaning out the old mess of calcium carbide. Electric lighting was obviously the ultimate, and it was equally obvious that an engine-driven dynamo should be capable of providing the necessary current. This ideal was only achieved in or about 1914, when the Indian twin featured a sophisticated electrical system that not only catered for all necessary lighting and ignition, but also turned the engine over to start with; this was done by a dynamotor which was wound to act as a dynamo at 6 volts or as a starting motor at 12 volts. This Indian was, at least in this respect, years and years ahead of its time, but other makes by

1906 $3\frac{1}{2}$ h.p. Quadrant (32)   1912 NSU (33)

40

Electric self-starter and dynamo on an Indian (34)

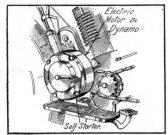

Electric motor and dynamo on Indian.

1914 had at least reached the stage of the dynamo. Before, electric lighting had been dependent upon accumulators or dry batteries.

The late pre-war Indian was not the only motorcycle of the period to be strikingly modern in conception. There were two others of equal distinction, both of them British. One, the ABC, was doomed to a very brief and not terribly successful life, although its design has been emulated by other makers since: the other, the Scott, not only preceded and indeed outlived the Indian but is, it is pleasant to record, not dead yet. Before we embark on a discussion of these two outstanding machines, however, it is imperative that we devote some space to what was without doubt the most important aspect of technical improvement in motorcycles of this period. Reference has already been made to the intractability of the old single-speed bicycles, to the difficulties involved in starting, stopping, climbing hills, negotiating hairpin bends, and so on. If the motorcycle was to become a practical mode of transport and a vehicle that could be managed without athletics, it was imperative that this situation be remedied. The first cautious experiments to this end were made about 1905, and they all had in common the continued use of the flexible belt drive. The simplest way of altering the gear ratio of such a set-up was to alter the size of the pulley on the engine crankshaft. By splitting the pulley so that one flange could be moved axially relative to the other, the effective diameter of the pulley could be varied and the speed range of the machine increased in the same proportion. By about 1908 there were a number of designs which allowed this variation to be performed while the motorcycle was in motion; but in 1911 (to be precise, during a single week in the month of June) the idea was taken a stage further by the Rudge Whitworth Company, who were faced with the need for providing adequate variable-speed transmission for the belt-driven Rudges entered by private owners in the Isle of Man Tourist Trophy Race. What Rudge did was to arrange for the engine shaft pulley to be expanded in contrary sense to the belt rim on the rear wheel, control over the system being exercised by a long lever alongside the fuel tank. The idea was to maintain constant tension of the belt, and this was achieved over a speed range of 1:1·73. This range was scarcely wide enough, and the complicated rear pulley looked clumsy, but the apparatus was a great popular success and the ensuing years saw large sales of the Rudge 'Multi', as the machine so fitted was styled.

Whilst the adjustable pulley had its adherents, a number of other designers preferred to provide a discrete number of speeds. NSU achieved this with simple efficiency by the provision of an epicyclic gear cluster built into the engine pulley and capable of being locked or freed to give two-speed transmission. This gear unit could in fact be bought and fitted to other motorcycles of single-speed belt-drive design. More common than the NSU two-speed device was the epicyclic hub gear, offering two or more speeds, such as still survives in some pedal cycles. Mechanically complex, these hub gears were rather too delicate for the brutal treatment meted out to them by the coarsely-running motorcycles of the day, so the separate countershaft gearbox was conjured into being by firms such as Fafnir or Chater Lea, whose three-speed gearbox of 1906 set a pattern for the future.

Unmistakably Scott—the radiator and line that for so long have distinguished these estimable machines (35)

42

Another type of two-speed transmission involved a pair of primary chains running on sprockets of different sizes, individually keyed or dog-clutched on to a countershaft from which the secondary chain drove the back wheel. The first motorcycle to embody this was the P & M in 1906; two years later Alfred Scott of Bradford produced his famous motorcycle with the same type of transmission, clearly copied from the illustrious example of his fellow Yorkshireman, who became properly incensed and sued him. The evidence given in Scott's defence made it clear that the idea was of immemorial antiquity and had in fact been used in not dissimilar form by Werner and by de Dion Bouton— which no doubt gave the Enfield firm all the encouragement they needed to use the same type of transmission in their models of 1910.

We have already commented on the tendency of Yorkshiremen to be, if not exactly idiosyncratic, at least somewhat original. Alfred Scott of Bradford was such a man. From the very beginning of the century he had been working along his own lines to develop the two-stroke engine, being by no means impressed by the harsh and fast-wearing single-cylinder four-strokes of the day. Scott's idea was a little parallel-twin two-stroke with the smoothness of torque of a four-cylinder four-stroke, and a perfection of balance that was hardly to be bettered. Scott owned a pedal cycle and sometimes he attached his prototype engine to it; he also owned a small boat, and as often the engine was put to work in that. The transmission system that he chose we have already described, but Scott took the idea a little further than his P & M model by pivoting one of the pedals (pedal gear was still used for starting) so that it could be used to pull the engine round by a length of chain—the first kick-starter. The frame for this bicycle was an open tubular structure laid out as a wide double cradle, not dissimilar to the old Hildebrand and Wolfmuller; the front forks were of the Rex type, the tubular fork blades sliding in guides to give motion analogous to that of the modern telescopic fork, but simplified by the adoption of a single central spring unit in front of the steering head. In 1908 the Scott machine came on to the market, built in Bradford by the brothers Jowett who attained a more lasting fame as manufacturers of light cars and cycle cars. In fact they only built the Scott motorcycle for a year, after which Scott made his own arrangements. The acceleration, the speed, the handling qualities and the sound of the Scott have become legendary, and were all amply demonstrated in the bicycle's early years by a string of brilliant competition successes.

Success in speed events distinguished likewise the A B C. Designed by Granville Bradshaw, this was a product of a new company that stemmed from the All-British Engineering Co. who built airplanes. Its design, featuring a duplex cradle frame of fully-looped disposition with trailing-arm rear suspension sprung by quarter-elliptic leaf springs, fairly conventional girder front forks similarly sprung, and a horizontally-opposed two-cylinder engine lying across the frame very low down, for all the world like a

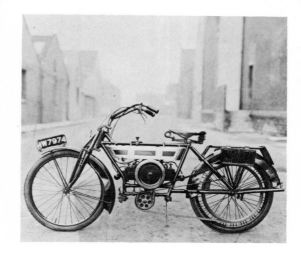

1911 horizontally opposed twin Douglas (**36**)

43

The era of the giant pulley, with a spare round the front forks. 1908 B A T (37)

modern B M W or Douglas, was perhaps the most modern of any to be built before 1935. Perhaps also it was better in conception than in execution, for it acquired a rather dubious reputation as far as reliability was concerned. There is no doubt, however, that when it went properly it went very well indeed: the 500 c.c. A B C set up a speed record at Brooklands in 1914 of 80½ m.p.h. After the war was over a 400 c.c. A B C was to do even better and to last even less time. How much power the 500 needed to achieve this speed is not known; but we do know that the 500 c.c. Rudge which in 1914 won the Senior T T in the Isle of Man had a maximum output of 13½ b.h.p., about three times the yield of touring engines of comparable size five years earlier.

Brooklands and the T T—two kinds of racing, two names particularly cherished by the British motorcycling enthusiast. Of course, not all significant racing was limited to Britain; but the two kinds epitomized by these two circuits were undoubtedly the most significant of the era. In the years from 1903 to 1914 motorcycle sport took on an entirely new form and a much amplified importance. While the century was still young there were the small-track races such as we have already described, and there were the great inter-city races, in which there were classes for two-, three- and four-wheelers. After the ill-fated Paris–Madrid race of 1903 a new type of race was organized over a closed circuit, and an international field was arranged by restricting the entries to teams of three from each country. Britain sent a Quadrant, a Lagonda, and a JAP; but they were as doomed as all the other foreign entrants to suffer from the chicanery and nobbling practised by the French hosts. The finally unchallenged victory of the French team was so transparent a piece of Chauvinism that the event was subsequently declared null.

Jack Marshall lapped the T T circuit at 42·48 m.p.h. in this 3½ h.p. Triumph in 1908 (38)

Opposite: Early American racing—on boards, at Speedway Park, Maywood, Illinois, 1915. *Centre:* on dirt in 1913. *Bottom:* against an aircraft at Wisconsin State Fair in 1915. Harley-Davidsons triumphant all the way (39, 40, 41)

44

Nevertheless the type of event became firmly established. Other types also grew in popularity, notably the long-distance reliability trial such as the Glasgow to London run, or the 1,000 Miles Trial. Long-distance record breaking over public roads also had its vogue, the standard course in Britain being from Land's End to John o' Groat's, covered in $41\frac{1}{2}$ hours in 1908. Then in 1907 the famous banked outer circuit at Brooklands was opened and it became possible to drive cars and motorcycles continuously at speeds as high as they were then capable of reaching. In that same year there was held in the Isle of Man the first Tourist Trophy race. The full mountain course had already been used for eliminating trials for the motor car race known as the Gordon Bennett Trophy and for the motor car Tourist Trophy race, but it was generally felt that motorcycles were not man enough for the full round-the-island mountainous circuit. A shorter and easier course was selected, and entries of touring motorcycles were invited. The definition of a touring motorcycle was rather vague: it was agreed that it should have two brakes and a silencer, a tool bag and a proper saddle; but more fundamental design features caused trouble. Fuel tank requirements in particular proved to be difficult to settle, until eventually it was decided (only in the month before the race) that there should be *two* races, one for two-cylinder machines and one for singles. The former would have to be capable of 75 m.p.g., the latter of 90.

In other respects the event was modelled on the International Cup races, with machines being sent off in pairs at regular intervals so that it was not exactly a race but rather a time trial. The single-cylinder race was won by a JAP-engined Matchless ridden by Charlie Collier, one of the pair of brothers who were to become famous in racing motor-cycles of this make. Ten minutes behind at the end of ten laps there came a pair of Triumphs. The race for two-cylinder machines was won by a Peugeot-engined Norton ridden by Rem Fowler (Rem was a diminutive of Rembrandt) and his win was much more conclusive, for the second-place Vindec was half an hour behind, with the third man a further twenty minutes behind him. Fowler's Norton was very much faster than any of the other 'bikes, and averaged 43 m.p.h. for one non-stop lap; but it had an awful spate of trouble with tyres and driving belts, reducing the overall speed to 36 m.p.h. as compared with Collier's 38.

Thereafter race speeds mounted rapidly. By 1909 the TT was being won at 49 m.p.h., this time by the other Collier brother, Harry. Both the Colliers featured in several events at Brooklands; in 1910 Charlie and Harry finished first and second in the Isle of Man.

A year later came a most important development in the history of motorcycle racing. The TT was revised and would in future be staged over the full-length circuit, including the stiff climb up Snae Fell mountain. It followed from this that effective variable gears would be necessary and, as we have already described, the Rudge Whitworth firm rose to this challenge with commendable speed. Nevertheless the 500 c.c. single-cylinder machines were again trounced by the twins, although regulations now limited the latter to a swept volume of 585 c.c. in an effort to keep the classes comparable. This appears something of a paradox today, when it is known that the twin is invariably more powerful than the single, *ceteris paribus*, but the situation in those days was compli-cated by the restriction on fuel tank capacity and the inevitably greater thirst of the twins. Be this as it may, the first three places in the race were taken by Indians, fol-lowed by the now traditional Triumph as the fastest of the singles. The Indians were of some technical interest, having two-speed countershaft gearboxes and all-chain drives; but the highlight of the event was the new lap record established by a Scott ridden by Frank Philipp, a cousin of Alfred Scott.

46

Technical discussion over a TT Rudge Multi (42)

The peerless Collier brothers, founders of the Matchless. *Above:* Harry Collier in 1911; and Charlie Collier before the 1912 Senior **(43, 44)**

Indian triumph. Paddock scene after the 1911 Senior (45)

50

Tyre trouble for a Rudge Multi (46)

Alfred himself had been doing quite a lot of competition riding since he first introduced his brilliant little bicycle in 1908. He had not the genius of his cousin, nor perhaps can he be considered in the same class as the most famous of the rider-manufacturers, people like Norton and the Colliers. But the invigorating acceleration and reassuring handling qualities of the Scott were excellent remedies for all kinds of shortcomings, and he did quite well in an assortment of hill-climb and sprint events—so well that the rest of the trade persuaded the recently-formed Autocycle Union as governing body of their sport to introduce regulations which hampered two-stroke engines in general and water-cooled two-strokes in particular. Other than the Scott there were of course no water-cooled two-strokes.

In making things difficult for Scott they gave him at the same time a perfect opportunity for some pretty thorough-going publicity, for there was no doubt that the new regulations could be interpreted as a recognition of the Scott's inherent superiority. Alfred was not the sort of man to miss such an opportunity. He was an interesting character in many ways, probably the most endearing of all the men whose greatness in the motorcycle world was attained in those early years. He was, as we have said, a Yorkshireman—which is a good start for all save those with Lancashire connections; unlike many of the somewhat rough-and-ready individuals who were to be found in motorcycling even then, he was a Public School boy, having been educated at Abbottsholme.

51

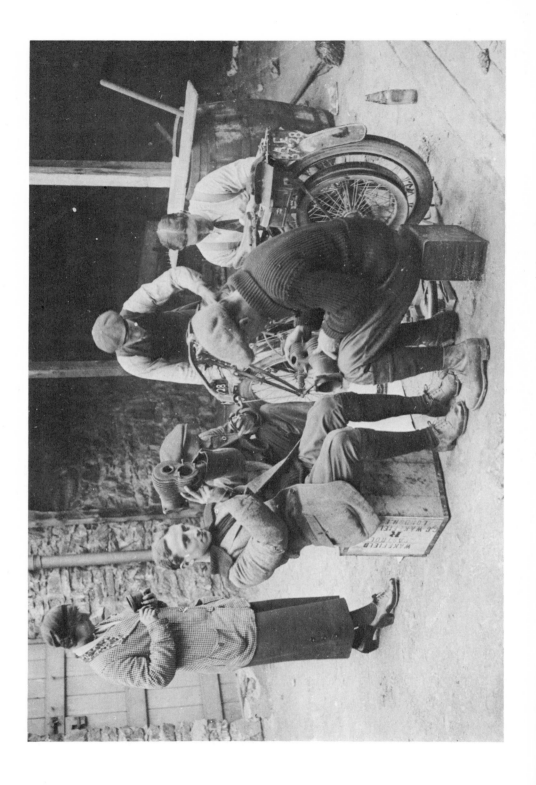

Two informal TT workshop scenes (47, 48)

This school had something of a reputation for developing free thinkers, but Alfred Scott was far from being a renegade. He was essentially a man of simple ways, content to pursue his ideals with as much dogged persistence as might be necessary before they might be realized. He was a perfectionist in matters of detail, as is testified by the carefully varied dimensions and extremely precise machining of the skirts of his pistons, and by the ridiculous ease with which it is possible to dismember a Scott engine, if necessary removing and replacing the big-end bearings by the roadside with little need for anything more than a small spanner or two. It may have been his insistance on perfection that caused him to remain a bachelor; but it is equally possible that this was the result of his being one of twelve brothers.

Whatever he was, Scott was not a wealthy man. After the withdrawal of the Jowetts from the original arrangements for manufacture of the Scott motorcycle, Alfred only managed to get going again with the assistance of friends and relatives. His company as eventually formed was scarcely to be reckoned with in the balance-sheet terms which are all that accountants understand of industry; but as a maker of outstandingly fast, safe

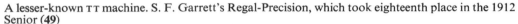

A lesser-known TT machine. S. F. Garrett's Regal-Precision, which took eighteenth place in the 1912 Senior (**49**)

Opposite: Tom Peek (Peelers) and W. Creyton (Ariel) going through Kirkmichael in 1913 (**50**)

Cyril Pullins on a Pastmasters in the 1914 Senior (**51**)

and satisfying motorcycles it was a force with which to reckon very seriously indeed. To win the two Senior T T races in the space of four years is an achievement still not so common as lightly to be dismissed: to do so with such meagre resources as Scott did was to enforce recognition as a doughty opponent for any manufacturer. The last T T win by a Scott was in 1913; in 1914 the same rider, Tim (H.O.) Wood, led from the start with a record 53 m.p.h. lap. Then the little Scott's Bosch magneto packed up, and the race was finally won by a Rudge Multi after the second fastest machine in the race, Collier's V-twin Matchless, had broken its frame.

It was a great race, and featured some splendid fights; but unfortunately for a lot of motorcyclists and for a lot of other people a greater and more calamitous struggle was soon to be begun by the world's leading powers, who would not desist until they were all exhausted and for ever confounded, four years later. In the meantime motorcycles and their riders found new jobs to do: communications being in their then somewhat immature stage of development, the despatch rider with his motorcycle was an important agent of military administration and strategy. All the principal nations used them, the British army favouring in particular the new model H version of the 550 c.c. Triumph single-cylinder side-valver with countershaft gearbox and chain-cum-belt transmission. The Royal Flying Corps went in for P & M mounts; and a number of other famous makes also saw service, notably the little 2¾ h.p. Douglas. Many of these models survived the war to return to production for Civvy Street. Sometimes they reappeared in modified form, sometimes virtually unchanged; but however the motorcycles themselves might have come through those momentous years, human life would never be the same again.

New Douglas opposed twin at Brooklands in 1914 (**52**)

Brooklands—as the artist saw it. *Right:* Charlie Collier flat out on his Matchless-JAP **(53, 54)**

57

Godfrey's Indian at Brooklands, 1911 (**55**)

Some 1914 technical features: Clyno quadrant-change. Rudge
controls. Early example of shaft drive. Oil bath on a Sunbeam (**56–59**)

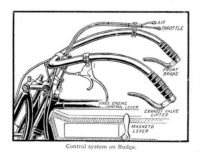

Control system on Rudge.

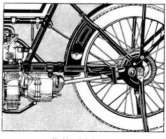

Working of shaft drive.

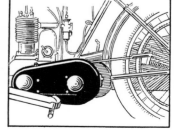

The arrangement of the Sunbeam oil bath chain cases.

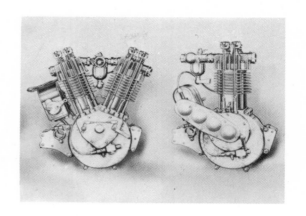

The heavy brigade. *Right:* 1912 Pope twin 1,000 c.c. and single 500 c.c. engines, which challenged the high output Harley-Davidson, Indian, Merkel and Emblem engines (**60**)

Below: 1913 1,000 c.c. Excelsior (**61**)

A pre-World War I sampling: The clean, refined Sunbeam; 500 c.c. V-twin Motosacoche; American Underslung Militaire; 1912 Bradbury (62–65)

In-line fours like the FN and Henderson were built for smoothness, not for speed (66)

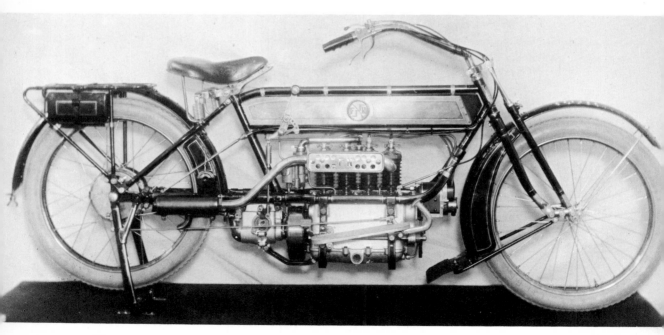

A sporting pair. Miss N. Cottle and Mr J. O. Watson-Bourne off for the International Six-Days Reliability Trials on their Raleigh (**67**)

The sale has been concluded. Father on his new 'combo' prepares to set forth, while the proprietor of the Viaduct Cycle and Motor Works is surely confident that the cheque will not bounce (68)

Side-car
Interlude
I

A modest sampling of the wide range of seating available for the family by 1914. Fresh air, and every comfort, were catered for, and nothing could have been more pleasant on a fine day and a smooth road. (The family is the Brunells. Father a prominent photographer of the motoring scene, and daughter Kit to be a famous rally driver in later years) (69–72)

Brooklands in 1911. An anxious trio make their faltering way up the test hill (**73**)

1916-1925
3 Reaching maturity

One moment in Annihilation's waste,
One moment of the well of Life to taste—
The stars are setting, and the caravan
Starts for the dawn of Nothing—oh, make haste!
Fitzgerald's first translation of Omar Khayyám

By 1919 motorcycling in America had almost died. The domestic motor car industry had learned the art of mass production so well that competition from absurdly cheap motor cars had left the many American motorcycle manufacturers with scarcely any market. One by one they went to the wall, after a few years of diminishing output and stultified design. Only Indian and Harley-Davidson remained as substantial protagonists of a two-wheeled way of life that even they had to modify somewhat if the last adherents were not to be seduced by the tempting four-wheelers.

This left Britain as the world's leader of motorcycling. Centre of the industry, nursery of the greatest riders, Britain was to enjoy henceforth a completely dominant position for several years. Motorcycling the world over took its pattern from the way British designers were thinking, from the side effects of British legislation, British weather, British empiricism.

At least British engineers had a lot of new things to offer after a war-time spell of frantic search for new ways to make more efficient machinery. The lessons learned were reflected not only in basic design features that found their way into motorcycles but also in the sheer quantity of models produced. All up and down the country there were industrial organizations with mass production capacity who were only too pleased to find some use to which to put it: so in 1919 more than a hundred firms offered more than 200 different types of motorcycle.

In their design, the lessons learned in the development of aero engines during the war were particularly evident. The rotary engines of the scout and fighter aircraft that had lately been disputing for supremacy in the French and Belgian air taught the designers a great deal about reduction of weight and size, about valve gear and cooling, about lubrication and metallurgy. In 1920 there was even a three-cylinder rotary engine of 309 c.c. produced by Redrup that it was proposed should be manufactured for motorcycle installation. It never caught on, but *The Motor Cycle* found little of which to complain when testing it.

This was not the only thing that the motorcycle manufacturers refused to accept from the aircraft industry. Magnetos with a rotating permanent magnet and stationary windings had become generally accepted for aero engines, being considerably more reliable; but motorcycles continued to be fitted with the older type in which the permanent magnet was the stator and the windings were wrapped round the motor—though, until modern coil or electronic systems took over, the magnetos of some of the best racers eventually became rotating-magnet instruments.

In other respects the post-war designs were markedly better than their pre-war equivalents. Virtually any motorcycle worth calling a motorcycle now had a countershaft gearbox and all-chain drive. The gearboxes were usually three-speed affairs allied to hand-operated plate clutches, but there were a few four-speeders. The lever to select the gears was usually mounted on the side of the petrol tank, sliding through a slot in the quadrant and located by notches in its various positions. There were kick-starters too, almost universal, so that the run-and-bump start became unnecessary. A certain amount of athleticism was still necessary in order to get the engine spinning, and the prospect of a back-fire still terrified every novice who was kick-starting a motorcycle for the first time in his life.

Just as a far larger number of people were mechanically minded by the end of the war than there were at the beginning, so was an understanding of electricity more wide-spread. This meant that there was a favourable climate for the growth of electrical accessories on motorcycles, so that the dynamo lighting systems that were being tried out in a half-hearted fashion in 1914 were now taking over almost completely. The particularly pinch-penny rider might stick to the older acetylene lamp, but gas-light could not endure long. In the 1920s a popular lighting system was to tap the primary winding of the magneto so as to draw off from it the unabsorbed half cycle there generated. This, of course, applied only to single-cylinder engines, but these were in the vast majority. This surplus current was led to a small battery and thence to lamps at front and rear; the lamps were never all that bright, for the total generating capacity was only about 3 watts, but speeds were not all that high and the illumination available was often sufficient.

Villiers, who had become quickly and firmly established as a manufacturer of cheap and trouble-free two-stroke engines available as proprietary units for an unholy rabble of cheap utilitarian motorcycles, developed the fly-wheel magneto for their engines. By slipping an extra coil into it, the alternating current generated could be fed directly to the lamps; later a battery was brought into the system by the simple device of adding a rectifier to the circuit so as to convert the alternating current to direct current.

Frame design remained completely stagnant. To be sure, there were one or two odd idiosyncratic men of genius such as Scott who produced motorcycles with frames which owed no more than necessary to the basic idea of the safety bicycle from the loins of which the motorcycle had sprung so many years earlier. In the majority of cases, though, all that happened to frames was that they grew heavier to cope with more powerful engines, heavier loads and higher speeds.

So much had speeds risen and so little had frames improved that in a few years the motorcycle was in much the same state as the motor car of the day; that is to say, the engine was too fast for the frame. The speed-wobble grew to be more dreaded than the side-slip; but this was not to happen for a few years. In the early 1920s the maximum speed of a typical touring 3½ h.p. solo machine would not greatly exceed 40 m.p.h., nor that of a side-car combination 30 m.p.h. Even this was illegal, for the speed limit was still 20 m.p.h. in Britain; but normal traffic on the roads travelled at higher speeds than this in perfectly reasonable safety, just as traffic today gets along comfortably at 10 or 20 m.p.h. faster than the antique speed limits to which we are subjected.

The power that provided all this relatively high performance came from engines that were considerably more advanced than their pre-war counterparts. Valve gear was often overhead, and the valves themselves now operated in a sequence which baffled the tyro because the inlet would open before the exhaust had closed. This overlap was the secret of efficient high speed breathing, and in those days was very mild, seldom amounting to more than a few degrees of engine rotation; but at least the germ of the idea had been sown. Lubrication was now quite commonly by pressure with the aid of a dry sump system, the used oil that fell to the bottom of the crankcase being pumped out to a

66

separate tank, a second pump drawing from this tank a supply of cooler oil to be delivered to all necessary points in the engine at a sufficient pressure. This was far better than the old 'total loss' system described earlier, which suffered from the comparatively slight disadvantage in those days that oil remaining in the crankcase got rather warm, but suffered much more from the ignorance and stupidity of a large proportion of riders who could not and would not take into account such factors as temperature, load, speed, and so on.

Most of these single-cylinder engines were still side-valvers, for this configuration had built up a reputation for good low-speed slogging ability and ease of maintenance and adjustment. The reputation was ill-deserved, but the motorcycling public of the day was not sufficiently educated to realize that the arguments were based on insupportable premises. At any rate, while the dodderers of the day clung to their side-by-side valves, the more progressive types were

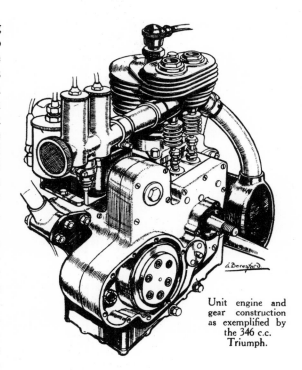

Unit engine and gear construction as exemplified by the 346 c.c. Triumph.

346 c.c. Triumph engine and gearbox (74)

buying o.h.v. affairs with the hemispherical combustion chamber that had been established as a classic in racing car engines by Henry in the years before the war. Valves were of larger diameter, pistons of aluminium alloy; and these design features combined with the more sophisticated valve timing to which we have already referred to make possible a considerable increase in crankshaft speeds and therefore in power. It was not long before the sportier singles were turning at speeds as high as 4,000 r.p.m. By 1922 J. A. Prestwich had introduced an engine with overhead camshafts, a morphological modification which produced still higher specific power outputs by making it possible for the valve gear to remain capable of efficient operation at a rate of rotation as high as 6,000 r.p.m. Even before then, Triumph had evolved with the aid of the late and great Harry Ricardo a pushrod-operated overhead valve design in which each pushrod worked a double rocker arm that opened two valves. As any Hondaphile of the 1960s will tell you, four valves are more efficient than two, all other things being equal, and this cylinder head design was a great success.

As has always been the case, there were one or two non-conformists about who resented that metallurgical monstrosity the poppet valve, and sought to achieve the workings of the four-stroke cycle by other mechanical means. Thus we had the Barr and Stroud sleeve valve, which combined reciprocating and rotating movements to cover and uncover ports in the cylinder wall. The difficulty, of course, was that differential expansion of cylinder, sleeve, and piston made it impossible to maintain the necessary clearances at all times, so lubrication and cooling were decidedly problematic and prevented the engine from being developed to a competitive level of specific performance factors.

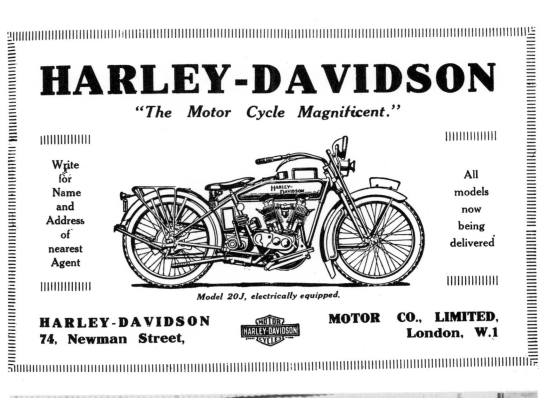

Unmistakably Harley . . . 1925 7/9 h.p., with side-car (**75**)

THE RIDER OF AN

Indian

MOTOCYCLE

always has the happy feeling of knowing that he is mounted on the best motor cycle ever produced

SEND FOR LIST

(76)

American machines in Britain. Harley-Davidson V-twin at Brooklands; and *above* Freddie Dixon, Indian-mounted, after his third in the 1923 Senior (*77, 78*)

1921 550 c.c. Indian twin (**79**)

All that has been said here about the single-cylinder four-stroke might be repeated twice over in summarizing the developments that were taking place in the design of the many V-twin engines that appeared on the market. However, a rather larger proportion of the twins had side valves, due to the popularity of this type for lugging side-cars about —remember that old chestnut about good low-speed pulling power. The few twins that had overhead valve location were generally considered as super sporting vehicles, and any bicycle boasting an o.h.v. JAP engine would undoubtedly qualify for the road racer category. Some Harley-Davidson and Indian twins of 1,000 c.c. capacity had four valves per cylinder but these machines were unquestionably track models.

Convenient though it was to install in the old-fashioned diamond frame, the V-twin engine left a certain amount to be desired in terms of balance and smooth torque delivery. The horizontally-opposed twin was still its superior in both these respects and continued to enjoy the particular attention of the Douglas firm down in Bristol. Their horizontally-opposed twin, with its cylinder axes disposed longitudinally, had been well established before the war, and had grown immeasurably more popular during it, thanks to its exploits between the knees of many a uniformed despatch rider. The pre-war Douglas racer had overhead valves; so had the post-war Douglas road machine. A number of other makes contrived engines of similar layout; but it was the ABC and later the BMW that demonstrated the ease of installing a flat-twin engine in a motorcycle by setting it athwart the frame. The BMW was made near Munich by the firm whose initials stood for Bayerische Motoren Werke—Bavarian Motor Works. The engine drove the rear wheel through a car-type clutch and gearbox and then—almost a wonder of the age—a shaft. This was sophistication indeed: practically every

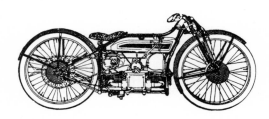

Douglas flat-twin sprint machine (**80**)

motorcycle going used chains, undoubtedly remarkably efficient when clean, new and nicely lubricated, but in their exposed position hardly likely to enjoy these circumstances for more than a few miles. To be sure, a few motorcycles such as the Sunbeam had featured extensive enclosure of the transmission chains, sometimes merely as protection against the dust and rain, sometimes devised as oil baths to maintain copious lubrication of the many over-worked plain bearings of which a roller chain is comprised. These enclosures, however, had proved unpopular, either because they rattled, or because they got in the way when a wheel change was necessary, or simply because they did not look sporty enough. Whatever the objection to them, they went; but with the BMW or older FN shaft drive there were no such problems. The gears built into the rear half might not display the same high mechanical efficiency as could a chain, but such efficiency as they had they kept.

The ABC was even more outstanding in its day. Designed by Granville Bradshaw in 1918, the engine was a 400 c.c. flat-twin of three nominal horse power, set with its o.h.v. cylinders across a remarkably modern-looking cradle frame. Built along car lines, the transmission comprised a plate clutch fitting on to the back of the engine's enclosed fly-wheel and linking it to a four-speed gearbox that had a car-type gate-change gear lever. Indeed, the only concessions to contemporary practice seemed to be the presence of a wheel at each end of the bicycle and chain drive from gearbox to rear hub. The frame

1921 ABC (**81**)

was sprung front and rear by slender pairs of quarter-elliptic leaf springs. There were internal expanding drum brakes on both wheels, and there was even a measure of protection against the weather. The bicycle was light, fast, and blessed with extremely good handling characteristics, which allowed the rider to exploit to the full the power developed by the lightweight and efficient engine (an engine which incidentally was to enjoy a fair measure of success in light aircraft). Just about the only real snag in the specification was the vulnerability of the cylinder heads and valves in the event of a spill, an objection that could also be raised to the flat twin from Munich.

The ABC was very successful in speed events, running off with a whole string of records at Brooklands and elsewhere. Alas, it enjoyed no similar success commercially. The manufacturers were the Sopwith aircraft firm who came out of the war with a big organization, well staffed, and with at least one factory that could be devoted entirely to the production of what was to be this popular motor cycle. At first it hardly seemed that things could possibly go wrong: the design was the talking point of motorcyclists everywhere they met, and with so famous a manufacturer backing it, surely it must be a sound proposition? Orders flowed in by the thousands; but the difficulties of design, testing, and getting production under way at the factory made themselves felt in delayed deliveries and gradually rising costs.

When the first orders were taken no prices were being quoted for the ABC. Eventually a figure of £160 was announced; but by this time most of the customers had gone elsewhere, and if they had not fared any better, they had at least managed more cheaply, for many machines of the day could be bought for £50 or so. True, the very next day they were liable to be three or four times as dear, because of the sudden wave of inflation that hit the country in about 1920, but at least the buyer had a motorcycle to show for his money. So the orders were cancelled, the customers disappeared, and so did all the capital that Sopwith had appropriated for this project. The bicycle itself was not yet really ready: better, they thought, to cut their losses. Production ceased.

James Sheldon has said of the ABC that 'only Bradshaw could have designed it, only Ford could have organized its production, and only Morris could have sold it on the scale necessary for financial success'. Perhaps the same might be said of the four-cylinder motorcycles that enjoyed a brief spell of popularity in the immediate post-war years. Best known in Europe was the Belgian FN, a 750 c.c. air-cooled in-line four coupled to a car-type gearbox and clutch, and enjoying such other four-wheeler attributes as wet sump lubrication and shaft drive. It did not remain on the market for many years, however. Europe indeed hardly seemed to be the place for four-cylinder machines —partly because (outside Germany) the Europeans were not particularly good at mass production and so not capable of producing such a machine at a reasonable price, and

74

1920 5 h.p. Zenith Gradua, a well-built J A P-engined V-twin. Note tram-handle control of the variable pulley transmission (**82**)

A Beautiful Machine—
designed by an expert for the use of riders who desire the very best.

The 1920 N.U.T. is the personal design of Mr. Hugh Mason. It is the concrete expression of his aims, and, with its Lucas electric lighting set, it forms a really fast, ultra-luxurious touring solo motor cycle.

THE NEWCASTLE-UPON-TYNE MOTOR CO., LTD.,
ST. THOMAS STREET, NEWCASTLE-UPON-TYNE.

PRICE 140 GUINEAS.

THE SEAL OF SUCCESS

(83)

ARIEL
THE DUAL VICTOR.

The machine that won the Team Prizes in both the English and Scottish Six-days Trials will be the centre of attraction at the Show.

STAND 47

You can't afford to miss it. Make it your mount in 1924.

Send for Catalogue.

ARIEL WORKS LTD., 3, BOURNBROOK, BIRMINGHAM.

(84)

Ace: American in-line four (**85**)

partly because the single-cylinder machines of the day were so effective in their environment. Only in America, where anything could be made cheaply without sacrificing too much in its specification, and where the added power of a big four was of real value on the long runs which that vast country made available, did the four-cylinder motorcycle engine endure. Best known was the 1,170 c.c. Henderson, but there were others including the Ace—which was also designed by Henderson and was eventually bought up by Indian and included in their catalogue.

If most European motorcyclists preferred to these Anakim a small and efficient single-cylinder four-stroke, there were nevertheless a large number of riders who were even more attracted by the mechanical simplicity of the two-stroke. The arguments put forward in favour of the two-stroke's greater reliability were more supportable in those days than they are now: the four-stroke's poppet valves were made of unsatisfactory materials, and the exhaust valve in particular would suffer surface deterioration with alarming rapidity. About the only thing a two-stroke suffered from was heavy deposition of carbon, but practically every engine suffered from that in those days.

Most of the two-strokes of the post-war era were simple and cheap affairs, either run up by some scant-brained mechanic or self-styled engineer in his back-garden workshop, or else produced in large quantities by firms like Villiers and Union for fitting to machines of all kinds. These two-strokes were all, of course, of the old-fashioned deflector piston type, with three ports cut through the cylinder and crankcase walls for induction, transfer, and exhaustion of the mixture in its various phases. But, as with frame design and engine layout, the two-stroke world had its ration of free-thinking radicals. Thus we found engines like the Dunelt, which appeared in quarter- and half-litre versions, each employing a stepped piston: the upper and smaller diameter section rode in the working cylinder which also formed the combustion chamber; while the larger-diameter section of the piston banged up and down in a lower compartment, displacing due to its greater diameter a relatively large quantity of air and petrol mixture and to all intents and purposes working as an induction pump or supercharger to give the engine higher volumetric efficiency than the crude two-strokes of the day normally enjoyed.

We have already noted some of the actual innovations that crept into motorcycles during this period, but it must not be supposed that the hastily-organized Olympia show at the end of 1919 contained much of note. Brakes were still more apparent than real, tyres were still skinny beaded-edge affairs, frames very reminiscent of earlier practice.

Harley-Davidson: American flat twin (**86**)

The beginning of the end. First the suffragettes, then the vote, then this. A final act of emancipation in 1925 (**87**)

ADJUSTABLE SPRING FRAME

Edmund

Bad roads *have* to be negotiated, and even though it were possible always to pick and choose your route, you cannot guarantee them otherwise. Does that mean that you must face discomfort in the saddle?—not a bit of it! In fact you can *depend* on absolute comfort all the time you are astride the

"Edmund" Spring Frame Motor Bicycle

and not even the roughest and most "pot-holey" of roads will convey to you anything resembling jar or jolt.

The action of the springs is, at all times, slow and steady, and they can be adjusted instantly to suit your weight exactly.

We have a leaflet fully describing the Edmund, and copy may be obtained either from us or any of the Edmund Agents.

C. Edmund & Co. (1920) Ltd.
Crane Bank, Chester.

BEARDMORE Precision MOTOR BICYCLE

THE Beardmore-Precision Motor Bicycle is intended for the rider who desires the fullest possible enjoyment and the least personal discomfort; who wants to use his machine every day and regards motor cycling as a pastime rather than as a feat of physical endurance; who prefers cleanliness to mere pace; who wants to feel that he has the best.

¶ *"Designed on novel lines with a new and apparently perfect method of lubrication. Its chief points are the luxuriously sprung frame, the petrol tank made from two steel pressings welded together and forming part of the frame, and the two brakes, both of which are really efficient."* *"The Daily Graphic."*

The Price is £95 Complete.   Particulars from

F. E. BAKER, Ltd., The Precision Works, King's Norton, Birmingham

" The Same as You can Buy."

Godbolds.

However, there was a surprising number of spring-frame designs coming on to the market, mostly employing a swinging rear fork whose pivot, at the back of the gearbox, gave the sort of suspension geometry that was only rediscovered and properly appreciated in the 1950s. Such a spring frame, with the springing medium itself being a pair of laminated quarter-elliptic leaf springs, was only to be expected on so advanced a design as the ABC already mentioned; but several other makers adopted a like system, including Beardmore-Precision, Matchless and Raleigh.

Another was Wooler; this was but one of a new generation of fore-and-aft cylindered flat twins whose engines were mounted relatively high to accommodate a gearbox beneath the rear cylinder, a practice also followed by Douglas, Brough the elder, Humber and Regent. The Wooler was to be distinguished from all these, however, both by the peculiarity of its suspension system, which featured short vertical plungers for both wheels, and by its long torpedo-shaped petrol tank built around and extending well in front of the steering head—a stylistic experiment which earned the Wooler the nickname of the 'flying banana'.

If there was a rash of flat twins, there was a positive plague of small cheap two-strokes. We have already described how Villiers and others had developed certain aspects of their engines and these were put into very large-scale production. Availability of an engine through the trade made it possible for large numbers of 'assembler' firms to set themselves up in business, occupying the most rudimentary premises and often possessing nothing more than a selection of spanners and some sort of working agreement with a local stove-enameller. To firms such as these engineering was a matter of buying the appropriate cycle parts from firms like Haden, or Sun, and simply putting them together. The engines might come from Dalm or Union—or from Villiers, who alone supplied more than 300 such firms at about this time. There were also, incidentally, firms like JAP and Blackburn producing $2\frac{3}{4}$ h.p. four-stroke singles in quantities that, if not competing with the two-stroke hordes, at least permitted distribution to a number of assembler companies.

However, it was AJS who really set the engine world alight by adopting the hemispherical cylinder head with wide-splayed valves, proved in the Peugeot racing cars of pre-war days. In 350 c.c. form this engine was installed in their racer for the 1920 TT, a racer that also contrived to have a six-speed transmission by a combination of three-speed countershaft and two-speed primary gears. Although a lack of team discipline caused the AJS protagonists to fight each other to a virtual standstill, the AJS proved to be considerably faster than the opposition, Derek Williams lapping the circuit at 51 m.p.h. The course had been altered for the event since the last race in 1913. The 1920 Junior TT was also notable for containing 250 c.c. entries competing for a separate cup awarded

Gallic brilliance. 1922 double overhead camshaft vertical twin Peugeot (**90**)

All roads lie open to the
Kingsbury Scooter

A thoroughly practical little machine, that will take you wherever you want to go—to little known beauty spots beyond walking distance, on by-roads which no car can traverse—that is the Kingsbury Scooter. It is designed for honest hard work and economical running. Easy to ride and easy to control, safe and speedy, it is the ideal mount for a country spin, a shopping expedition, for sport or business.

Engine.—2 h.p., 2 - stroke.

Ignition.—C.A.V. Magneto.

Transmission. — Enclosed Chain Drive to back wheel via countershaft.

Lubrication. — Automatic.

PRICE:
40 Guineas.

LONDON AND MIDLAND
MOTORS, LTD.,
445, Oxford Street,
LONDON, W.I.

Telegrams. "Lonandmid, Wesdo, London."
Telephone - - - - Mayfair 1304.

by *The Motor Cycle*. The same thing happened in 1921, paving the way for the new light-weight 250 c.c. race to be introduced in 1922.

Continental Grands Prix were won by the French Gnome et Rhône—which was the ABC built by them under licence and bored out to 500 c.c. It was probably this machine, which soundly trounced the vertical twins from Griffon and Peugeot, that inspired BMW (taking to motorcycles after starting life as aero-engine makers) to adopt the transverse-engine layout with longitudinal crankshaft.

This period also witnessed a short-term flurry of motor-scooters, many of them surprisingly like those that we know today. They all had small engines, some of them two-strokes and some o.h.v. four-strokes. They were made by firms like Quadrant, ABC, Kingsbury, Reynolds and sundry other even more obscure names. Sometimes both wheels were sprung, sometimes neither. Sometimes there was no saddle: indeed this was a popular configuration, for the scooters of the day were never intended to be ridden fast, and for a mere trip up the road to post a letter why sit down? Because the scooter of the day was conceived as being so short-distance and utilitarian a vehicle, it was of utmost simplicity with a mere single-gear transmission. This very simplicity was its downfall, for it failed to be competitive with the motorcycle proper and cost far more than a push-bike.

At the remotest possible pole from these rudimentary two-wheelers was another type of machine which, built privately in very small numbers in 1919, went into more substantial production in Nottingham in 1920. The manufacturer was George, son of

The golden age of the Brough. 1924 at Brooklands, E. C. E. Baragwanath with side-car, and, of course, sporting a wing collar (**92**)

84

THE 1924 "S.S. 80" MODEL
Brough Superior

(The original Sporting British Big Twin).

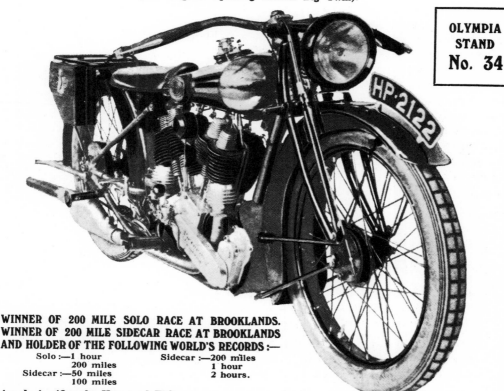

OLYMPIA
STAND
No. 34

WINNER OF 200 MILE SOLO RACE AT BROOKLANDS.
WINNER OF 200 MILE SIDECAR RACE AT BROOKLANDS
AND HOLDER OF THE FOLLOWING WORLD'S RECORDS :—

Solo :—1 hour	Sidecar :—200 miles
200 miles	1 hour
Sidecar :—50 miles	2 hours.
100 miles	

Amply justifies the Honoured Title :

"THE ROLLS ROYCE OF MOTOR CYCLES."

(vide " The Motor Cycle," Nov. 1922).

It is the most luxurious mount ever produced, and its specification includes :—

The sweetest running and most powerful Motor-cycle Engine ever produced incorporating a fool-proof system of Mechanical Lubrication
Original and protected Design of Loop Frame.   Original and protected Design of Steering Head with Steering
   ,,   ,,   ,,   ,, ,, Saddle Tank.   Damper incorporated.
   ,,   ,,   ,,   ,, ,, Twist Grip Controls.
   ,,   ,,   ,,   ,, ,, Quick Detachable Rear Mud-   Original and protected Design of Adjustable Handlebars.
                guard and Carrier   ,,   ,,   ,,   ,, 3-Jet Single Lever Carburettor.
Lucas Magdyno and Electric Horn as standard, Three-speed Gear Box with Close Second and Top Gear Ratio, Alternative positions of
Footrests, Internal Expanding Brakes, Front and Rear, Ground Clearance 4½", Saddle height 26⅜", Cylinders can be removed with Engine
in situ, the Steering and balance at the highest possible road speeds are unequalled.

Brough Superior After—delivery—Service is unique. Ask any Brough Superior Rider.

GEORGE BROUGH, HAYDN RD., NOTTINGHAM.
'Phone : 2782 Nottingham.
'Grams : Brough 2782, Nottingham.

William E. Brough, an established manufacturer of flat-twin motorcycles. Young George, who had spent part of the war working on the development of aero engines at the Coventry factory of White & Poppe, fancied the idea of producing a big machine of really top-notch quality. His father did not, so George Brough prised away his one-third share in the partnership which existed between him and his father and set himself up in Haydn Road, Nottingham, as manufacturer of the Brough Superior.

That first machine was powered by an engine specially built by J. A. Prestwich, and often referred to as 'the ninety bore' on account of its cylinder dimension, the stroke being appreciably shorter. It was a V-twin with light-alloy pistons, while all the overhead valve gear and the lower portion of the cylinders were heavily plated. The same attention to finish was evident in many other parts of the machine, and appearances were notably studied in the shape of the petrol tank, with its distinctive bulbous nose and unusual saddle arrangement, straddling the top tube of the frame to provide the utmost capacity; its $2\frac{1}{2}$ gallons of petrol and $\frac{1}{2}$ gallon of oil were by no means excessive for a thirsty big twin.

Bearing in mind the poor quality of the petrol of the day, motorcycles were reasonably economical thanks to their light weight, high gearing and moderate performance. However, the vagaries of carburettors in those days undoubtedly resulted in some waste—Setright remembers a JAP-engined Morgan three-wheeler, the fuel consumption of which he improved from 20 to 35 m.p.g. simply by substituting a modern Amal instrument for the original and admittedly somewhat worn Brown & Barlow. George Brough evidently was conscious of the mixed feelings entertained about vintage carburettors even in the days when they were contemporary, as we may judge from this paragraph in the specification of the early ninety-bore Brough:

CARBURETTOR. A special type of multiple jet AMAC two-lever instrument is fitted as standard. Opinions on carburation are divided, and the maker is willing to fit any other make of instrument to order.

It is also worth extracting the last paragraph:

When considering the price of the Brough Superior, remember that the maker never intended to produce his design as cheaply as possible. It is a machine made to cater for the connoisseur rider who will have the best and fastest machine on the road.

Here at last was a man catering for the requirements of a special class of motorcyclist, one that had been slow to grow, would never reach large proportions, and would slowly die away. The motorcyclists of the real pioneer days had been largely men in the trade, augmented as time went on by a sprinkling of sons from what were by the standards of the time reasonably well-to-do families. After the war the upper and middle classes preferred to see their sons in motor cars, and since the sons themselves could not fail to see the advantages of a four-wheeler as a means of conveying the gentler sex, the preference was one to which they readily acceded. In consequence motorcycling was growing to be a proletarian activity.

Nevertheless there remained a sizeable number of gentlemen, young and not so young, who regarded poodle-faking and the weather protection of the motor car with scorn. Believing that 'he travels fastest who travels alone', they managed to satisfy themselves—if nobody else—of their sturdy masculinity by bestriding a good lusty motorcycle. However, their standards were high: they demanded good performance, good looks, lasting reliability and a high standard of finish. There were not many machines

Watercooled!! Scott

WRITE FOR ILLUSTRATED BROCHURE AND NAME OF NEAREST AGENT TO -

The Scott Motor Cycle Co. Ltd.   SALTAIRE. YORKSHIRE

(94)

that could satisfy them: the long-stroke Sunbeam was one that did, the Scott another—though Alfred Scott himself had sold out in 1919 for a reputed £52,000, leaving as his successors a group of devoted Yorkshiremen who strove to maintain the same standards. But for the most discriminating rider of the '20s with enough money to indulge his tastes, the obvious choice was the Brough Superior. If that did not satisfy him, nothing would.

The Brough Superior's performance may be summarized by saying that from 1920 onwards George Brough and many private owners notched up a tremendous list of successes in competitions, both in reliability trials and in speed events. As for the smoothness, capability, quietness and high standard of finish, let the reader if he is competent to so do muse on these qualities as displayed by the Rolls-Royce Silver Ghost, and then consider the fact that by 1921 the Brough Superior was becoming known as the Rolls-Royce of motorcycles. This appellation was sparked off by a letter from a customer, published by Brough in a leaflet describing his machines, saying: 'I certainly think your machine is the Rolls-Royce of motorcycles.' In the following year the *Motor Cycle* said: 'One would have thought it impossible to add any further refinements to the ss80 Brough Superior. Yet this Rolls-Royce of motorcycles—it earns the title by something more than mere cost—has been further improved. . . .' Such comparisons are not lightly permitted by the august officials of Rolls-Royce, but Brough contrived to obtain their approval of the reference.

The manner of his doing so, however, makes an amusing story that is not widely known. Apparently there descended upon the Nottingham works one day an exalted individual from Derby who made it known that Rolls-Royce were somewhat concerned by the reference in George Brough's advertising. Brough promptly took the gentleman off on a works tour, conducting him first into a room where two white-coated men in white gloves were fussing over the fit and finish of the petrol tank on a machine that stood resplendent as few others before or since. Taking in this impressive sight, the Rolls-Royce official pronounced himself more than satisfied that the Brough Superior was manufactured to standards such as the Derby firm themselves recognized, and departed a happy man. George Brough, displaying all the tact obligatory among gentlemen, forbore to explain to him that the men he had seen were top-grade fitters preparing an exhibition machine for the Olympia show!

There were not many who could afford or who could justify the expense of a Brough Superior. However, there were several other big twins coming on to the market, and not by any means were all of them American. For example there was the handsome and fast Martinsyde, a 750 c.c. machine built in Kingston-upon-Thames by Martin and Handasyde, who had made some rather splendid-looking aircraft during the war. They were not the only aircraft firm to be engaged in motorcycle manufacture, but they were less unsuccessful than the others. More big twins were available from Matchless with JAP or MAG engines and sprung frames, and from BSA who introduced a 770 c.c. big twin at the 1919 show.

In general, however, the big single held sway, with the 350 AJS hammering around the Isle of Man in 1921 to win not only the Junior race, which on the previous year's form was only to be expected, but also the Senior, giving away 150 c.c. while contriving to average 74 m.p.h., a speed faster than the speed of the Sunbeam that won the Senior race in 1920. Nevertheless, it was Sunbeam who won the 1921 French Grand Prix, the new 'long-stroke' model being the last of the successful racing side-valvers and relying as much upon the virtuosity of rider Alec Bennett as upon the lively but deceptively smooth performance which made this model popular for many years.

Scotts-men. Jimmy Simpson, before the 1922 Senior; and *below* Harry Langman, so loyal for so long to this make, at the first Ulster Grand Prix (**95, 96**)

Graham Walker, fourth on a Norton in the
1923 Senior (**97**)

The great Alec Bennett (number 11) at the
start of the 1925 Senior (**98**)

One of the most illuminating sets of race results from 1921 is the list of finishers in the 500-mile race at Brooklands. This marathon of the oval track was won by an Indian ridden by one of the most outstanding big twin riders of the era, Herbert Le Vack—whose idea it was to fit Castle forks, with their bottom-link suspension characteristics, to the front of the Brough Superior, where they remained on practically all subsequent models. Second to Le Vack was motorcycling's iron man, Freddie Dixon, riding another big twin, this time of Harley-Davidson manufacture. Winner of the 500 class and fourth fastest overall was a side-valve Norton which contrived to average 62 m.p.h., eight less than Le Vack but six more than Coventry Victor or Martinsyde could manage in the 750 class. Even the little side-valve New Imperial did better than 50 m.p.h. to win the Lightweight class.

Perhaps the biggest surprise was the 52 m.p.h. victory of a little single-cylinder two-stroke Ivy which cleaned up the Junior class; for some reason it did not have to contend with any of the formidable o.h.v. AJS team. The other sensation of the race was provided by the Ricardo-engined Triumph, described at the beginning of this chapter. In the early stages of the race the machine was troubled by a slipping clutch, and the trouble was rectified too late; once it had been seen to, however, the Triumph re-entered the fray, running for lap after lap in company with Le Vack's winning Indian, though the latter had twice as much engine.

J. A. Watson-Bourne (Triumph) glances behind at Indian-mounted Freddy Dixon in the 1921 Senior: they finished fifth and second respectively (**99**)

Stanley Woods with his
Cotton-Blackburne in 1923
(**100**)

C. W. ('Paddy') Johnston,
similarly mounted, after
placing second in the 1925
lightweight (**101**)

The names of Le Vack and New Imperial were coupled in the following year, when he led for more than half of the Junior TT, with a pack of seven AJS riders raging impotently in his wake. The beautiful New Imp had a JAP engine that was to set two long-lasting fashions. In the first place it had two exhaust pipes, both leading from the same exhaust valve—a mere conceit that stayed with the o.h.v. single until the end of the late 1930s. In the second place, its overhead valves were operated by overhead cams driven from the crankshaft by a shaft and bevel gears. As we have seen, the qualities of the overhead camshaft layout in permitting the use of high rates of engine revolution and of valve acceleration had been known to the makers of racing car engines for many years. Among the quantity manufacturers, however, both of cars and motor cycles, a barely supportable legend became established that the overhead camshaft engine was excessively noisy and costly to produce. It took the example of Honda to enable us to take the layout for granted in an ordinary touring motorcycle.

Quite a number of features made their first appearance in the years between 1920 and '25. For example there was the Research Association disc brake fitted to the TT Douglas for 1923. The Duggie was ridden to victory by a local man, Tom Sheard, the first Douglas win since 1912—and incidentally both races were marked by dreadfully wet weather. The course was slightly different, having been modified again in 1921 and '22, since when the route has remained unchanged—although the subsequent improvements in road surfacing have in themselves been responsible for vast increases in speed.

One of the most interesting machines to appear in 1922 was the Ner-A-Car, a highly unconventional design from the board of an American named Neracher. Made by Sheffield-Simplex, it had a long, low, pressed-steel frame which carried within it any of a variety of engines, most commonly a 285 c.c. two-stroke. Transmission was by a peculiar friction drive, and there was hub-centre pivot steering. Whether due to this steering, to the low centre of gravity, to the long wheelbase, or to a fortuitous combination of all three, the Ner-A-Car was blessed with superlative steering qualities. It could be ridden to a standstill feet-up, in a way that made the best of trials machines look ungainly; and it was equally sure-footed when being ridden at high speed with the rider's hands off the handlebars. Setright has a friend who used one in those days for commuting between his home and his father's woollen mill, a trip that he would make comfortably seated and reading a newspaper, the Ner-A-Car responding beautifully to a slight body lean which was all that was necessary to make it go where it was required. On one occasion he failed to see over the top of his evening paper his father's car being driven in the opposite direction, the subsequent stern paternal wigging causing a change of mount.

Neither the hub-centre steering of the Ner-A-Car nor the primitive disc brakes of the Douglas were destined to survive. Rover, however, who produced a lightweight in 1923, endowed it with a unit-construction engine gearbox assembly which set a pattern that after a decent interval (thirty years seems to be a typical gestatory period for any motor-cycling novelty) became recognized practice.

By this time the market was in the hands of the buyers rather than of the sellers. Prices had dropped to a level little higher than obtained before the war, bearing in mind the inexorable decrease in the purchasing power of the pound. The lightweights could be had for well under £50 and one of them, the 'built like a bridge' Francis-Barnett, cost only £27. This was the first of the 'Fanny' Barnetts to have a fully triangulated space frame, built up from small-diameter tubing bolted together in such a way that all the tubes were free of bending loads. There had been triangulated frames before, of course, notably that of the Scott, but never a fully triangulated one. The Francis-Barnett was a strictly

Comfort and stability endowed the Ner-a-Car with great charm (**102**)

utility bicycle with a 150 c.c. Villiers two-stroke engine and a two-speed gearbox. Another cheap (£37) two-speeder was the 250 c.c. round-tank BSA, a side-valve machine that sold in vast quantities. Such a shortage of transmission ratios meant that the engine had to have a lot of pulling power over a wide range of speeds; but the champion in pulling power was still the Brough Superior, George Brough riding his side-valved 'Old Bill' to 51 wins in 52 sprint events during 1923.

The following year went down in history as Norton's year of firsts: it was scarcely before it was due, for they had not won a TT since 1907. In 1924, though, Nortons won the side-car race in the Island and also the Senior TT at 62 m.p.h.—a new record. Nortons also won the French, Belgian and Ulster Grands Prix, the Senior class in the Brooklands 200-mile race, the Spanish twelve-hour race, the Circuit of Cremona, and many more, in the hands of riders such as Alec Bennett, Joe Craig, and Tazio Nuvolari, later to become the world's greatest car-racing driver. Nortons made a great deal of advertising hay from the fact that the machines raced were precisely the same as those sold to the public, a claim that could not perhaps be made for the six-speed big-port AJS which nevertheless put in a record Junior TT lap of 65 m.p.h., considerably faster than any of the Senior machines could manage.

F. C. North with BSA, 1921 (**103**)

All this frenetic scratching around a rider's circuit might prove any of a variety of things, but to prove which was the world's fastest motorcycle called for a different approach. This was provided by Brough Superior the following year, when they introduced their new model, the ss100, powered by a new 980 c.c. JAP V-twin with pushrod o.h.v. and hemispherical combustion chambers. Herbert Le Vack rode the Brough to take the world solo and side-car records at 123 and 103 m.p.h. respectively. The Brough had already acquired a new loop frame the previous year, and its saddle tank was getting well enough known for the more style-conscious designers to take note.

What really started the saddle tank on its long career, however, was the HRD, a make which was new to the world in 1925. The initials were those of Howard Davies, who had won the Senior TT on an undersized AJS in 1922. His own new machine was a 500 single aimed at the quality market: it had a duplex cradle frame, and a tall JAP engine of 490 c.c. made yet taller by its pushrod-operated overhead valve-gear. The only way to keep the tank reasonably low and maintain its accustomed relationship to the ridiculously low saddle that was then fashionable was to use a deep saddle tank that fitted astride the frame's top tube and the valve gear and bulged out on each side to provide the necessary tank capacity. One or two other manufacturers of big singles, Montgomery and Chater Lea, did likewise; the HRD, however, found itself more distinction by winning the Senior TT at 66 m.p.h., a new record and convincing evidence of the good handling qualities of the bicycle.

This may have mattered at the time, but hindsight suggests that the HRD's most important contribution to motorcycling was that it started the saddle-tank fashion which was to be adopted by all manufacturers within three years, and brought to an end the era of the long, low, lean-tanked vintage motorcycle. Even Wooler abandoned its 'flying banana' tank, and about the only motorcycle left looking as it always had done was the Scott. Scott's latest in 1925 was the Super Squirrel, now available in 500 or 600 c.c. sizes and looking not dissimilar from the older three-speeder or even the early two-speeder. But, dash it, the 1965 Scott doesn't look all that different, and there is probably no very compelling reason why it should!

The beginning of a new era. The first Moto Guzzi (**104**)

Side-car
Interlude
II

Some of the grace of the early 'cars was lost in the 1920s, but weather protection (*see over*) improved (**105–6**)

*For Solo
and Sidecar.*

97

(107)

Freddy Dixon won the 1923 Side-car TT with this Douglas 'combo', remarkable for the banking side-car wheel lever-controlled by the passenger (108)

'Combo'-expert E. C. E. Baragwanath at Brooklands (109)

1923 big-twin Harley-Davidson outfit (**110**)

1926-1935
4 The classical era

Change and decay in all around I see.
H. F. Lyte

In the chronicles of motorcycling the decade from 1926 to 1935 is not a remarkable one. The period began in the booming, uproarious 1920s, but a few brief months of explosive decompression were to kill its effervescence when the stock market crashed on Wall Street in 1929, followed by similar slumps in Britain, France and elsewhere. In 1935 motorcycle design was in the melting pot; but in 1925 it had crystallized after more than a quarter of a century of experiment and conjecture. The intervening ten years, that all too brief hiatus stretching from 1926 to 1935, may be looked upon as the vintage years of the motorcycle, the classical era when evolution had come to a halt and revolution had yet to intrude. To the motorcyclist everything seemed to be for the best in this best of all possible worlds, in which all motorcycles were the same, but some were better than others.

The classical motorcycle was one of three kinds: there were the gentle-natured and persevering side-valver of moderate capacity, the crackling o.h.v. single of not more than half a litre displacement, and the noble big V-twin—plodder, pacer, and patrician. In all these power was available in abundance, and indeed was by now too great for the frames of the time, whose steering qualities caused the dreaded 'speed-wobble' to figure increasingly in accident reports. But, if the engine was usually 10 m.p.h. faster than the bicycle, so to speak, the bicycle itself had at least come a very long way from its humble origins and was now a considerably more highly-developed structure without yet suffering from excessive weight. At all normal speeds the bicycle was light and easy to handle, responsive, mettlesome perhaps; but so long as the niceties of the friction damper on the steering head were understood, so as to avoid the tank-slapping handlebar shimmy of the high-speed wobble, it was a machine that was easy to control. Standards of finish were high, prices reasonable, and the roads generally good enough and empty enough to make motorcycling a pleasure any time and anywhere.

In America motorcycling had succumbed to the temptations of the cheap mass produced motor car, and there was little use for the two-wheeler except as a tool of law enforcement. Britain ruled the international motorcycling scene, and its plethora of motorcycle manufacturers enjoyed a domestic market that must by far have exceeded that of any other country. In 1926 this was a matter for smug self-congratulation; but in the Isle of Man in 1926 the writing was already on the wall for those who could read.

In the Lightweight TT of 1926 an Italian rider named Ghersi put up a brilliant performance that left all the field gasping in his wake. You will not see his run recorded in the annals of the race, for he was disqualified under a new rule that required all equipment carried during the race to be identical to that used during the practice sessions. Ghersi, alas, ran his Guzzi during the race on a different sparking plug from the one that was fitted at the weigh-in; and the officials, concluding that a new rule must be enforced to the letter if it is not to suffer disrespect in the future, disqualified him. The ensuing uproar made it clear that this was considered a thoroughly unsporting attitude to adopt; but after a while it transpired that Ghersi had been warned in advance that he was liable to infringe the rule and suffer disqualification, but had made it clear that as a visitor he expected to be given special treatment. All was well for the English then—the fellow had clearly tried to pull a fast one, and that was no way to behave among the sporting English! The firm of Cotton were doubtless particularly gratified since it left their machines taking the first three places, albeit at a speed considerably slower than the Guzzi's fastest lap of 63·21 m.p.h. In fact, the race was won outright by Mr C. W. (Paddy) Johnston. In the Senior and Junior races the respected names of Woods, Handley, Bennett and Simpson (a quartet of riders who were legendary in their time) filled the leading places on Norton, Rex-Acme, AJS and Velocette respectively.

The happenings during TT week of 1926 make a worthwhile study, and an interesting prelude to the ensuing ten years. The Junior race was outstanding, Alec Bennett on the overhead camshaft 348 c.c. Velocette finishing ten minutes ahead of the next man in a race otherwise notable for the fact that it was one lap longer than previously and was confined by regulations to ordinary fuel rather than dope.

Considered as a whole, the TT field was not distinguished for reliability, for only half those who started succeeded in finishing. An analysis of the specifications of all those competing betrays the variety of established practice and advanced technique always to be found in the racing world. Six models had dry-sump lubrication systems, in which oil was scavenged from the crankcase by a pump that delivered it to a large-capacity separate tank, from which another pump delivered it under pressure to those bearings deemed to need it. This was a considerable advance on the wet-sump system common in cars, and immeasurably more modern than the total-loss lubrication system upon which many production motorcycles relied. The AJS might be singled out as having no mechanical pump, but at least that make had already made a major contribution to engine design in its introduction of the valve gear and cylinder head described in the preceding chapter.

As to valve gear at the 1926 TT, it might be observed that the Rudge and the Guzzi each had four valves to grace the single cylinder head. Four machines had enclosed pushrods, and no less than five had adopted overhead camshafts. These five were Velocette, Guzzi, Bianchi, Matchless and Chater Lea—which last was particularly unusual in having a face cam rather than the radial type more commonly to be seen. The Bianchi had a modernistic frame with twin top and down tubes, and the beautifully finned and sculptured engine employed a train of gears to drive its two overhead camshafts. It was the little 250 Guzzi, however, that attracted most attention among those with technical interests. The machine was entirely new: a single-cylinder type, the engine carried its cylinder barrel horizontally, with a bronze cylinder head facing forwards to make the most of such cooling air as came eddying past the front wheel. The valve gear for this cylinder head was, as we have said, operated by an overhead camshaft; the valves themselves were closed by hairpin springs. Furthermore, as yet another sign of future times, the gearbox was in unit with the crankcase.

There was a 500 c.c. Guzzi in the Isle of Man that week as well, similar in general but distinguished by having more valves. It crashed and was never a force with which to reckon. Another Italian machine must have been formidable merely to look at: it was the Garelli, a split-single with four carburettors—a multiplicity which made it all the more unfortunate that a throttle wire should break during the race, forcing the rider to retire.

Brilliant two-stroke. 1926 DKW (111)

Coventry-Eagle with pressed-steel frame at the 1927 Olympia Show (112)

In Germany there came on to the market the 250 c.c. Patria, an overhead camshaft machine, and the 173 c.c. water-cooled two-stroke DKW, complete with a piston-type supercharger. New too were the 350 Schüttoff, an unremarkable pushrod job, and the big V-twin Mabeco which, with two exhaust ports and pipes for each cylinder, was described in the pages of *The Motor Cycle* as 'no longer a copy of the Indian Scout'—pictures suggest that it had at least as much in common with a Wagner tuba!

Some of the trends evident in racing machinery were to be displayed again at the motorcycle show at Olympia late in 1926, when the models for the following year were exhibited. There were more sports models with two-port engines, the pair of fat exhaust pipes issuing from either side of the cylinder head providing a corpulent symmetry that greatly appealed to the riders of the day. There were fewer four-strokes under 200 c.c., and at the same time there was a tendency for small two-cylinder machines to appear, whether two-stroke or four. Among the twins were to be numbered several new jobs of 680 c.c. capacity; and of these much the finest was of course the new 680 Brough Superior, apishly imitated by a Coventry Eagle that looked very much the same except for the girder forks that positively shrieked 'fake!' to anyone accustomed to the elegant Castle forks of the Brough.

The Brough had had this type of forks since early in 1925 and, to quote the Brough Superior historian Ronald H. Clark, 'the very term "Castle forks" suggests to the con-

Continental racing. 1927 Dutch Grand Prix, with Wilmot Evans (Triumph) in the lead (**113**)

noisseur hairline steering and cornering as if the wheels were flanged and running on rails at any speed; deflection was reasonably limited, and so very positive compared with the spongy overrated fittings called forks today. Other factors to be reckoned with are that the trail of a Castle fork remains constant and there is practically no alteration in the wheelbase when the fork is working. With ordinary girder types there may be an appreciable variation in the wheelbase adversely affecting cornering at high speed.'

Thus equipped, at a distance to divine the evolutions of the front wheel upon the road and to dictate its course, the rider of the 680 Brough Superior of 1927 had the pleasure of sitting astride what amounted to a miniature of the ss100. Instead of the big 1,000 c.c. V-twin of the full-blooded Alpine Grand Sports or Pendine models, the 680 had a derivative of the side-valve JAP engine of 674·4 c.c., adapted to overhead valve gear, and installed in a frame whose wheelbase was reduced to 56 inches. The machine would do 80 m.p.h. solo and with belt-driven Magdyno cost 103 guineas, compared with the £165 of the Pendine.

Brough Superiors and power were erroneously supposed to be almost synonymous; but there were other ways of providing plenty of urge than through the agency of a large o.h.v. engine. On the Douglas stand at the 1926 Olympia show was to be seen a 350 c.c.

1927 TT Sunbeam (114)

George Brough himself (*standing*) with Joe Wright (115)

side-valve Douglas (the famous EW model) fitted with a supercharger, a device in which a number of manufacturers were beginning to take an interest. On the increasingly large proportion of motorcycles enjoying overhead valve gear there was an increasing tendency to enclose it and the pushrods. Other trends evident were the use of duplex or single loop frames instead of the old pedal-cycle-inspired diamond pattern, while there were also more four-speed gearboxes and more dry-sumping of engines—better lubrication was becoming as evident amidst production machines as amidst racers.

Internal expanding brakes were now general, if not generous. Their smallness was excused on the grounds of weight-saving, for no manufacturer was going to admit that the wheels of his machine were so seldom in contact with the ground that larger and more powerful brakes would have done more harm than good. The wheels themselves were increasingly of the well-base rim pattern with wired-on tyres inflated to lower pressures than had previously been the rule; but there were still plenty running on the older-fangled beaded-edge tyre.

It was J. A. Prestwich and Co. who pioneered the overhead camshaft engine. In 1924, two years after the experimental TT 350 and 500 c.c. overhead camshaft machines, Velocette followed with their brilliantly successful Junior. The most outstanding of all overhead camshaft motorcycles appeared in 1928, when Norton's CS1 racer of 500 c.c. made its début. Like the Velocette and most other o.h.c. engines, the Norton motor had a single camshaft on the cylinder head, driven from the crankshaft through bevel gears and a vertical shaft alongside the cylinder. The method was not universal, however, for chain drive had its adherents as well—notably AJS when eventually they took to an

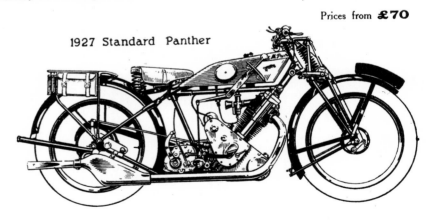

A MODERN MASTERPIECE

THE 1927 E.W. MODEL

Douglas

MOTOR CYCLE
Manufacturers by
Appointment to
H.M. THE KING

**WEAR A
FLANDERS POPPY**

Twenty years ago, before motor cycles had become established as a means of transport for the public, the first DOUGLAS engine was produced. The originator of its type—the horizontally opposed flat twin—it sprang to almost immediate fame, but so unorthodox and different was it from the recognised type of engine that a speedy doom was predicted for it. However, history proves that instead of dying out it became more and more popular, and to-day those desirous of keeping in touch with the development of the motor cycle engine are assured that the engine of the future is a MULTI-CYLINDER engine. DOUGLAS thought of this 20 years ago and still maintains this opinion.

The latest 1927 Models are a tremendous improvement on anything yet produced, and as the range covers every class of mount from the Standard Touring to the 100 m.p.h. Racing Models, the demand is even greater than ever.

The E.W. Models have firmly established themselves by their amazing successes in open competition and the 1927 Models proudly carry the title :—

"Still Leader of the Pack."

Model E.W. 3·48 h.p. 3-speed all chain drive, fitted with flywheel clutch and kickstarter, balloon tyres and low pressure brakes.   **WRITE FOR A CATALOGUE NOW!**

£42:10

Lamp, Generator and Horn 30/- extra.

SHOWROOMS :
39 Newman Street, W.1.
Tramway Centre, Bristol.

SERVICE DEPOT :
Oxford Mews Titchborne Street,
Edgware Road, W.2.

DOUGLAS MOTORS LTD., KINGSWOOD, BRISTOL.

(117)

overhead camshaft for their famous 7R 'boy's racer'. However, production engineers persisted in their heresy that overhead camshafts were by their nature noisy and expensive, so this form of valve operation was never widely adopted among road-going designs, although we shall later be referring to such exceptions as the early Square 4 Ariel.

If the overhead camshaft was exotic, the pushrod o.h.v. arrangement was almost invariably acceptable. Despite the astonishing performances of a Hartley-tuned side-valve Ariel at Brooklands, where the main object of the exercise appeared to be to demonstrate the advantages of alcohol as a fuel, no machine with any pretensions to high performance would have its valve gear anywhere but in the cylinder head. Sometimes it might be exposed, sometimes decently covered; but in either case the clatter from it was almost certain to be transmitted up through the petrol tank which shrouded it, to assail the ears of the rider until his speed was so high that the noise was carried away by the wind.

Except for the comparative few who chose to ride like that, the slogging old side-valve single-cylinder engine was just as popular. It was available in practically every common size up to 600 c.c. or thereabouts, and with its low compression ratio, gentle valve timing, small-bore carburettor and heavy flywheel, it was an extremely forgiving type. Easy to start, thanks largely to the modest compression ratio that was seldom more than 5:1, allowing easy kick-over, easy to handle in the traffic of the day because of its outstanding flexibility, seldom capable of outright speed sufficiently high to incur any special dangers, and most accessible for maintenance, the single-cylinder side-valve engine endeared itself to all but the rabid speed enthusiast. Superficially it might not have improved much in the course of the years that had passed since it became common for both valves to be mechanically operated; but in fact the improvements were great.

It was in better machining, better assembly and above all better materials that the superiority of the contemporary four-stroke lay. To be sure, there were detail modifications to the design that also brought benefits of various kinds: for example, cylinder heads were now detachable instead of being integral with the cylinder barrel, and this made the all-too-frequent decarbonizing and valve grinding job much easier. A valve chest had grown on the side of the cylinder valve, closeting within it the tappets, valves, stems and springs, to protect them from dirt and grit, and to ensure that the oil intended for their benefit would in fact reach them from the crankcase. The lubrication system itself, now of the dry sump type with mechanical pumps, represented a great improvement over the old plunger or drip-feed total-loss systems. Sometimes the gearbox was even built so as to be bolted directly on to the back of the crankcase instead of being a separate entity somewhere down along the frame.

It was above all improvement in materials, we must repeat, that was most responsible for increases in performance and reliability during this period. Aluminium alloys had been adopted gradually as the best materials for pistons ever since the Bentley rotary aero engines had demonstrated their effectiveness in scout aircraft during the war. The manufacture of piston rings benefited from improved iron-founding techniques, and scraper rings to control oil consumption began to supplement the compression rings on many pistons. This in turn reduced the oil consumption and, by limiting the pumping of oil from crankcase up to cylinder head, reduced the formation of carbon. Thus it became possible to run six or seven thousand miles between decokes, where once a thousand miles was as much as could reasonably be expected. The use of aluminium alloys also spread occasionally to cylinder heads, which with more liberal finning

The NEW
1927 16-H, 490 C.C.

Norton
(Registered Trade Mark)

The new 1927 Norton 16H, 490 c.c. Side Valve Model, is already in greater demand than its predecessors. No wonder. Look at the numerous improvements. Here is a machine, better than ever before and

Still the Same Price

Other Nortons for 1927 have been improved too, and most models considerably reduced in price. Even better machines than those that won most of the worth-while events of 1926—and at the remarkable prices here listed.

Norton Motors Ltd.,
Bracebridge St., Aston, B'ham.

1927 Prices:

Model No.

Model			
16H.	490 c.c., 3-speed	£59	10
1.	633 c.c., 3-speed	£63	10
14.	633 c.c., 4-speed	£68	10
18.	490 c.c. O.H.V., 3-speed	£69	0
34.	490 c.c. O.H.V., 4-speed	£74	0
21.	490 c.c. O.H.V., 3-speed, Dry Sump Lubrication	£74	0
19.	588 c.c. O.H.V., 3 speed	£72	10
24.	588 c.c. O.H.V., 4-speed	£77	10
44.	588 c.c. O.H.V., 4-speed, with 'Big Four' frame	£78	10
25.	490 c.c. O.H.V., T.T. Replica, 3-speed	£80	0
17C.	490 c.c. Colonial	£61	10
2.	490 c.c. Touring	£60	10

Sidecar Prices remain as hitherto.

(118)

allowed better cooling, and therefore higher compression ratios and higher volumetric efficiency, which is in turn a measure of specific output. Reliability and durability were also promoted by better steels which at long last showed signs of being matched to the job that had to be done by the hard-worked poppet valve, which has always been something of a bottleneck in four-stroke engine development. Thus, regrinding was less frequently needed, the engine held its compression better, valves were less liable to stretch or to hammer themselves pockets in the valve seats, and so valve timing in itself remained more consistent and the performance altogether more predictable.

All these material benefits were free for enjoyment not only by the old side-valver but also by all the other types of engine that were being developed during this period. The type that saw more development work than any other was the two-stroke. Already famous names like Scott and Villiers had established the fact that the two-stroke was not less practicable than the mechanically more complex four-stroke engine; however, it seldom yielded an acceptable performance. This was largely due to shortcomings in its breathing, and these were overcome by a rapid sequence of developments that took place principally in Germany.

It was in Germany that D K W took the first step—already recorded in this chapter—of introducing a separate cylinder acting as a charging pump, and capable of delivering mixture either at atmospheric pressure or with some degree of supercharge. In either case the result was aspiration that was considerably more positive than could be expected when relying on the original concept of compression in the crankcase during the downward movement of the piston.

This was far from being the major contribution made by D K W. Undoubtedly the most important was their adoption in 1929 of the loop scavenge system of Dr Schnuerle. This system was characterized by a piston whose top was substantially flat, instead of being built up in the form of an asymmetric deflector. The inlet ports were angled into the cylinder walls in such a way that the stream of mixture taken in during the induction stroke rose up the cylinder and, travelling across the combustion chamber, proceeded down the other side of the cylinder following the path of the exhaust gas escaping through its conventional piston-controlled port. The Schnuerle system at once showed itself far more efficient than the old deflector-top piston, yielding greater power, improved flexibility, and more consistent firing. It gave some scope for development, for the precise shape and location of the ports could only be determined after considerable experiment. D K W was not the only firm pursuing this end, for they were joined by Victoria, Zündapp and Villiers.

Meantime the Austrian firm of Püch had adopted the split-single type of two-stroke (already built for cars by Trojan in England) in which two adjacent cylinders shared a common combustion chamber and crankshaft. By means of articulated connecting rods, the crankshaft worked pistons in each of the cylinders slightly out of phase with each other, the differential motion thus induced allowing a valuable phasing of the opening and closure of inlet and exhaust ports. Thus the exhaust port would open first in one cylinder, to be followed shortly after by the inlet port opening in the other cylinder; approximately half a revolution later the exhaust would close, to be followed promptly by the inlet; and this was a sequence of events that could not be arranged in the conventional single-cylinder two-stroke. Were it not for the limitations imposed by the inconvenient shape of the common cylinder head and the severe differences in temperature existing between one side of the engine and the other, the split-single two-stroke would undoubtedly have been a greater success than it was. At any rate it caught on in sufficient

114

(119)

115

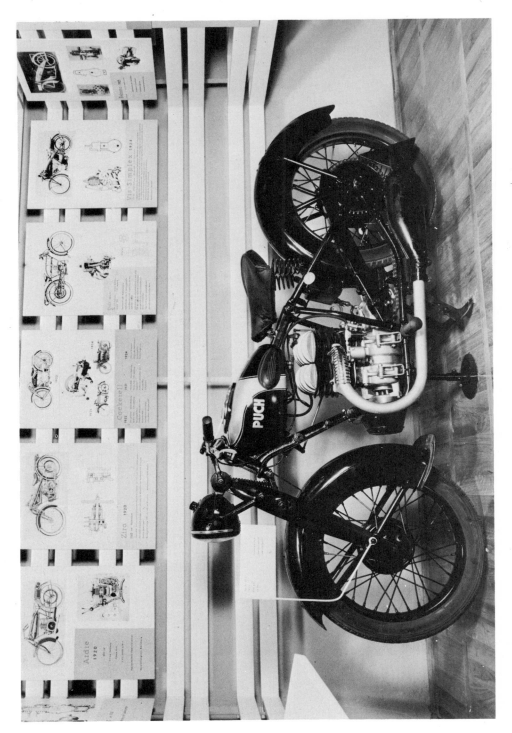

1931 Püch (120)

116

numbers to be pursued as a design ideal for several years, in fact surviving well into the 1950s.

The fact that small and mechanically simple two-stroke engines could be made in sizes as small as 100 c.c. made it easier to produce ultra-lightweight machines of great and utilitarian simplicity. This might have led to a resurgence of the scooter movement, but instead it brought about an adaptation of the pedal cycle in a particularly heavily-built form: with a small two-stroke of perhaps 98 c.c. slung beneath or in the region of the bottom bracket, and driving the rear wheel through a clutch and chain (there was no gearbox to complicate the issue), the autocycle was born, to remain in production throughout the period under review.

In this decade carburettors became slightly less difficult to manage, as the old two-lever instruments (one lever controlling the admission of air to the engine, the other the supply of fuel) virtually gave way to the so-called 'automatic' instruments in which the proportion of air to fuel was maintained at or near to the correct 12:1 proportions by weight throughout the whole operational gamut of the engine. It followed automatically from this that a simplification of the control could be adopted, so after the popularization of such carburettors as the Cox-Atmos or the Villiers, there was a general standardization on the use of a twist-grip throttle control by about 1930.

At about the same time we saw the last of the beaded-edge tyres, virtually completely supplanted by wired-on versions fitted to well-base rims. Tyre sections themselves became greater, but this was demanded in any case by the rapidly increasing weight of motorcycles. The increasing load meant that there was still no reserve of pneumatic cushioning to take the place of springs: and so we find some instances of the sprung frame in some Brough Superiors, all HRDs and one or two oddities such as the OEC. This last was more distinguished for its occasional marriage to the Temple front forks which, by means of some most unusual geometry, contrived to combine the suspension characteristics of telescopic forks with the virtues of hub-centre steering.

Another machine to exploit hub-centre steering and a fully-sprung frame was the Wallis, made in very small quantities and raced to no little purpose at Brooklands. The frame design was a most unusual triangulation of steel tubes arranged to form a shallow punt, from which a superstructure rose to embrace the steering head, and other extensions provided the locations for the swinging forks in which both front and rear wheels were carried. The springing media were laminated quarter-elliptic springs fore and aft.

More from the Continent. *Above:* 250 c.c. Ganna; and Belgian FN (**121–122**)

This decade also saw an almost complete change in the location and *modus operandi* of the gear-change lever. The original place for such a lever was in a quadrant on the right-hand side of the petrol tank. Gear-changing involved throttling down with the right hand, squeezing the clutch lever with the left, moving the gear lever with the right hand, re-engaging the clutch with the left, and opening the throttle again with the right. This was cumbersome, slow and inaccurate, and any sporting rider of reasonable skill would dispense with the clutch and make his gear changes simply by relying on accurate throttle control to effect the appropriate synchronization of engine speed to road speed for whatever gear was to be engaged: the right hand remained on the throttle and the left hand reached across the petrol tank to work the gear lever. Once this had been recognized it was but a short step to arranging for the rider's foot—usually the right foot—to work the gear lever, and the whole idea was made possible thanks to the invention of the positive-stop device that first made its appearance on the racing Velocettes. No longer did the gear-change lever move to a separate place for each gear: it was simply prodded downwards to engage the next highest gear and would then spring up to its original position, whence it could be prodded down again for another change up. A change down through the box would invoke hooking the toe under the pedal and raising it through a similar distance. Sometimes the directions were reversed according to the whim of the manufacturer, while in Italy there arose the practice of having a long pedal pivoted at its centre so that all gear changes could be undertaken by a downward movement either of the toe or of the heel. For no very apparent reason this never caught on in Britain, but proved extremely popular in Italy, where perhaps the finer climate encouraged riding in ordinary clothing, the footwear part of which would suffer if the toe of one shoe were scuffed by frequent hooking upwards of a gear pedal.

In fact gear-changing was not indulged in nearly so often in those days as has since become the case. Engines were still flexible and fairly soft in tune, largely because of the limitations of the petrol then available. But if the engines were open to generalization in these terms at least there was tremendous variety in other respects. There can hardly have been a time when engines came in more different shapes and sizes: *The Motor Cycle* in 1935 described seven types of British 'multis': there were the Douglas flat twin, the Triumph vertical twin, the normal V-twin, the Matchless V4, the Ariel Square 4, and the Scott two- and three-cylinder varieties. All these were running in parallel, as it were, and all had their adherents.

The horizontally opposed two-cylinder engine was not the exclusive domain of Douglas, although this firm continued to go from strength to strength in developing their little fore-and-aft flat twin in side-valve and o.h.v. versions and in every guise from the sedate tourer to the hairy racer or speedway machine. In Germany BMW had been pursuing this type of engine as well, and had already gone away from the longitudinal arrangement of Douglas in favour of the transverse disposition of the engine as pioneered in the British ABC. In the late 1920s and early 1930s BMW developed their machines in shaft-driven forms of various sizes and types, making themselves a fast-growing reputation for high quality and high performance. Their touring machines were abetted in this by sporting and racing mounts of high output and notably good handling qualities. There is no two-cylinder engine that runs as smoothly and as coolly as the transverse flat twin, and these properties, together with the high power output of which the BMW was capable, stood the Bavarian firm in very good stead for many years.

Douglas themselves emulated the layout at long last in 1935 when they evolved their prototype machine named 'The Endeavour'. This was a 500 c.c. side-valver, with the

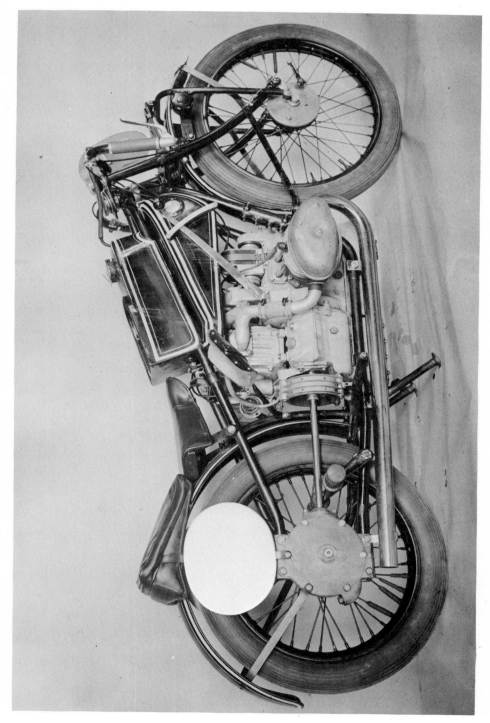

The formidable supercharged BMW of 1926 (123)

horizontally opposed cylinders set across the frame and driving through the gearbox a shaft which communicated to bevel gears on the rear wheel. The frame itself was a cradle type, very wide so as to lend some protection to the vulnerable cylinders.

To most motorcyclists, however, the word 'twin' meant the V-twin. There were V-twins in abundance, usually big and woolly affairs used for hauling side-cars or carrying hefty passengers over arduous touring routes. Most of them were simple giants with side-valves and precious little in the way of mechanical elaboration. There were some exceptions, notably the overhead valve JAP engines which were to be found in Brough Superiors and also in sundry other machines with pretensions to high performance. Over in the USA, Harley-Davidson and Indian continued to produce V-twins in large and very large sizes, their racing versions continuing the practice of having four valves to each cylinder.

In Britain JAP were not the only people making big V-twins, for Anzani were in the business as well; nevertheless the appearance in 1928 of a P & M Panthette V-twin of a mere 246 c.c. capacity came as something of a shock, almost a heresy, to the motorcycling world. Just to make matters worse, the engine was of unit construction with the gearbox and the cylinders set across the frame!

As time went on, though, it became clear that the big V-twin was either to be a really hefty side-valver with power delivery tending towards steam-engine characteristics, or else a fairly lively o.h.v. job of somewhat smaller size, sometimes as little as 500 c.c.— as for example the New Imperial and BSA.

Probably the most important development in two-cylinder engines in this period was the evolution of the vertical twin, in which the two cylinders were notionally separated by an angle of 360 deg., so that they were parallel to each other. The arrangement provided an extremely compact layout, and by mounting the crankshaft transversely across the frame it was possible at once to enjoy the traditional transmission arrangements which had become sanctified in conventional single-cylinder engines and to ensure that both cylinders got plenty of cooling air. By arranging the crankpins so that the two

1934 500 c.c. New Imperial for the TT (124)

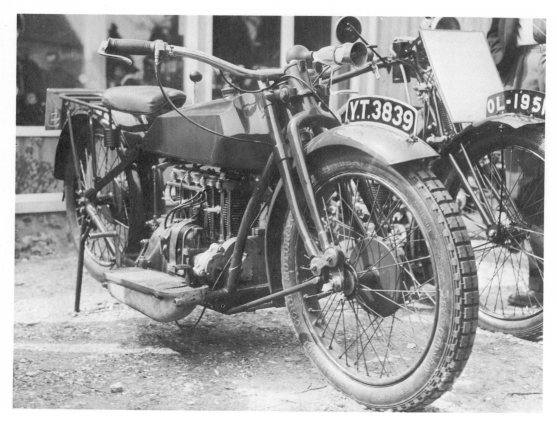

The pleasing four-in-line Vauxhall with traditional fluting (**125**)

cylinders fired alternately, an extremely smooth delivery of torque was assured; but at the same time perfection of balance was sacrificed, for instead of the two sets of recipro-cating weights balancing each other as they do in a horizontally-opposed twin, they simply went up and down together, so that the vertical twin was no better balanced than a single. Since the engine was so smooth in torque delivery, this vibration was in any case less apparent; and since in all other respects, notably easier starting, greater power output (because of increased rotational speeds and piston area), a more musical exhaust note and a quicker response to throttle opening, the vertical twin was notably sweeter and more responsive, the engine caught on in a very big way.

There is no doubt that the Triumph twin was the model that set the vertical twin on its feet: appearing in 1935, it was designed by Turner, who had come to Triumph from Ariel where he had been responsible for the Square 4 that we shall shortly be describ-ing. The earlier Triumph 650 was morphologically similar to the famous Speed Twin: it had overhead valves working in hemispherical combustion chambers, it carried its crank-shaft in two main bearings with a large bob weight between the two crank pins. But Turner's Speed Twin was much more compact and sweetly revworthy, and was destined to retain for decades its 1935 bore and stroke (63×80 mm.) which gave it a total swept volume of just under 500 c.c. Its performance, in terms of acceleration and maximum speed, was quite outstanding for its day, especially for a pushrod engine, and it was rather quieter than others of comparable power.

Having referred both to the Triumph vertical twin and to the P & M transverse V-twin, it is only fair to make some mention of an engine that came somewhere between them in appearance, although technically it was undoubtedly a V-twin. This was the Matchless Silver Arrow, of 1929. The two-cylinder engine was of 400 c.c. capacity, and the two cylinders were set at a narrow included angle of only 26 deg., so narrow that it was possible to combine them in a single casting set longitudinally in the machine's cradle frame.

In opposition to this school of thought there was the very wide-angled V-twin built by Guzzi. This 500 c.c. engine had its cylinders set at 120 deg. to each other, with the front cylinder horizontal and occupying much the same position in the frame as did the single-cylinder of the 1926 racing 250. With this low horizontal cylinder pointing forwards and the second cylinder sloping backwards, the centre of gravity was kept very low and there was plenty of room for circulation of cooling air. How successful this machine was we shall see towards the end of this chapter.

In the meantime we must move on from two-cylinder machines to those with three cylinders. One would scarcely expect three-cylinder engines to enjoy any very great popularity, and indeed since the unmourned passing of the radial in such forms as the Redrup (1920) there had seemed little likelihood of any engine appearing with such a number. It was perhaps appropriate that the convention-disdaining Scott firm should come along in 1935 with a new and elaborate three-cylinder in-line engine. It was something like a car engine to look at, or even a locomotive engine; very smooth and sheer in its flanks, water-cooled of course, and with a complicated crankshaft built up from a number of webs and pins running in ball and roller bearings. This arrangement allowed separate crankcase compartments for each cylinder, so as to permit the crankcase compression normal to the unsupercharged two-stroke. Built on to the back of the engine were a car-type clutch and three-speed gearbox, and it is recorded that the bicycle as a whole, whether despite or because of its very long wheelbase, was a delight to ride. The maximum speed was not particularly high, but the acceleration was satisfying and the flexibility quite extraordinary, especially for a two-stroke. In fact it seems there was nothing wrong with the three-cylinder Scott other than the fact that it cost too much: but in 1935 that was quite enough to damn it, and it never went into commercial production.

A rather better fate was enjoyed by the various new four-cylinder engines that made their appearance round about this time. Actually, things did not look too good for the four at the beginning of the decade under review: in 1926 FN, who had been building in-line-four machines almost from time immemorial, suddenly changed their policy and abandoned the four in favour of a rather utilitarian side-valve single. In the USA, where prosperity and long distances combined to make it desirable that a motorcycle should have as many as possible of the characteristics of the car (which most self-respecting Americans would rather have anyway), the four-cylinder machine remained in favour and the big Henderson went from strength to strength. Emulating it were the smaller Cleveland, a mere 600 c.c. affair, and the slightly bigger 1,229 c.c. Ace—which was in fact designed by Henderson and was fated to be taken over in 1927 by Indian. All these machines were much the same, heavy side-valve affairs which made some appeal for police work at a time when for one reason or another American police were being kept particularly busy.

By contrast, the four-cylinder machine in Europe, and particularly in Britain, was something produced in small numbers by, and for, idealists. Since the *beau idéal* of most

Fast
Foreigners

1930 Husqvarna, off to break Swedish records on ice—on a 16-inch back wheel (126)

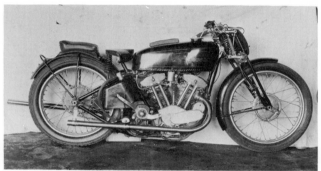

1934 Husqvarna, for the Senior TT (127)

1935 750 c.c. BMW, which took flying kilometre World Record at 256·064 k.p.h. (128)

1933 500 c.c. Husqvarna at Brooklands (129)

123

The big American Ace, later taken over by Indian (130)

riders of the time was the Brough Superior, it is scarcely surprising to find George Brough turning his attention to the four-cylinder concept; but the manner of his so doing caused an occasional eyebrow to be raised.

His first effort was a narrow-angle V-4 in 1927. Brough had originally intended to adopt the patents of the Italian car firm of Lancia, but was prohibited from doing so. Instead of having the narrow 20 deg. included angle between the cylinders that characterized the Italian car engine, the Brough V-4 was a 60 deg. affair, whose single camshaft nestled in the angle between the two banks of cylinders. The engine was a side-valver of 994 c.c. and proved no more of a success than it deserved. In the following year Brough had another go, this time designing an in-line four-cylinder engine that was built for him by the Swiss firm, Motosacoche. It was by the standards of the day a handsome engine, somewhat monolithic and simple in its exterior, with black cylinder finning and a ribbed exhaust manifold of aluminium, polished so that it shone prettily and was poor at shedding heat. Neither this machine nor its predecessor was immune from cooling troubles, for while the front cylinders received a reasonable draught of air, those at the rear had to follow along in the wake of the others and inevitably tended to run rather hotter.

It may be because of this that Brough's third attempt at producing a four-cylinder machine was to employ a water-cooled engine: this time it was none other than the Austin 7 car engine, somewhat modified. By the time Brough had finished winding the

124

EVERY Riding Need!

Every riding need is met in the "P & H" range of
motor cycle lamps and accessories. No matter what
your individual taste may be, there is a "P. & H"
model to suit. And . . . in each item you will find
a standard of quality which is unexcelled, a sound-
ness of design that is unequalled and a keenness of
price which yields the maximum value for any
outlay! Ask your dealer to show you
these "P & H" lines . . . you'll be
astounded at their outstanding quality
and value.

P&H

125 F.S.

FORK SPORTS SETS
offer an unobstructed road view and a
steady light, as all shocks are absorbed in
the Front Forks. Adjustable Brackets to fit
any make of Motor Cycle.
No. 120 F.S. 5 in. Front and 3½ in.
GENUINE MANGIN MIRROR.
Complete with No. 121 Generator **21/6**
No. 125 F.S. 5½ in. Front and 4 in.
GENUINE MANGIN MIRROR. With
No. 119 Generator **29/-**
No. 127 F.S. 6½ in. Front and 5 in.
GENUINE MANGIN MIRROR.
No. 124 Generator **46/-**

Reg. No.
236365

No. 180
PILLION FOOT REST
A great asset to passenger
comfort. Strongly made and
perfectly rigid. Fitted to both
chain and seat stays it cannot
move round into wheel or
chain. Adjustable to suit all
motor cycles and to fit on
either D shaped Per
or round tubes. pair **5/-**

No 212. **SPORTS HORN**
Of attractive design and sturdily constructed
for long service. Possesses a clear and
penetrating note. Will fit ⅞ or 1 in. Handlebar
and has a universally adjustable
bracket. **10/6**

No. 135. **THE POPULAR
TAIL LAMP.** The best
value of its type on the
market. 1⅝″ Red Glass, 1¼″
White Glass, N.P. or
Ebony & N.P. mounts **3/-**

P&H Ltd
POWELL & HANMER Ltd
BIRMINGHAM

1932 Jawa with odd trailing link front suspension (**132**)

frame about here and there in order to accommodate this awkwardly-shaped power unit, and tacked on some adiposity in the form of hefty electrics including a battery of no less than 42 amp hours capacity, the machine was fit for nothing except lugging platypode side-car outfits, a miserable duty in which it was to some extent aided by the fitting of twin rear wheels spaced just a few inches apart.

The four-cylinder Broughs, then, were deservedly unsuccessful freaks; but there were other British manufacturers who had not lost their touch, nor their eye for beauty. For example, Matchless followed on from their narrow-angle Silver Arrow twin to produce the Silver Hawk, a quite beautiful 600 c.c. overhead camshaft engine whose four cylinders were set at an included angle of 18 deg. in a single casting, topped by a detachable cylinder head carrying all the valve gear. No more compact four-cylinder engine could be conceived, and therefore none could be more suitable for incorporation in a motorcycle—always provided that provision be made for ducting cooling air to the rear pair of cylinders. The Matchless did not stay in production for long, although those who are lucky enough to have ridden one are usually loud in praising it. Perhaps its most outstanding virtue was its sweet and quiet manner, which gave the lie to the idea that any overhead camshaft engine was bound to be a noisy beast.

A rival design of almost equal compactness, but of considerably longer life, made its appearance in 1929 in the form of the original Ariel Square 4. This 600 c.c. engine had

126

four vertical cylinders, arranged in square plan in an air-cooled one-piece casting, surmounted by a detachable cylinder head which again carried overhead camshaft valve gear driven by a chain from the timing case on the off side. Heavier and more bulky than the Silver Hawk design, the Ariel was nevertheless better balanced: two separate crankshafts were used, each with a pair of crankpins set at 180 deg. to each other and the two crankshafts being geared together by helical teeth machined in the peripheries of their central flywheels, so that the two crankshafts were phased 90 deg. apart. The result was an engine whose four firing impulses were evenly spaced through two revolutions, and whose mechanical balance was well-nigh perfect—far better than that of any V-4.

The 'Squariel', as it became known, grew to enjoy a long and successful commercial life, as we shall subsequently see; but the 746 c.c. Nimbus four, built in Denmark, lasted for very little time. This had an air-cooled in-line engine built in unit with clutch and gearbox and equipped with overhead valve gear. The frame into which it was fitted was an open pressed-steel cradle, neither complex nor heavy—indeed the whole machine weighed about 380 lb., which was no more than the average for 500 c.c. single-cylinder machines of the time. Whether for want of a market or for want of adequate cooling for the rearmost cylinders, the Nimbus disappeared. It was not from Denmark but from Italy that the most significant four-cylinder motorcycle was to emanate.

This was the Rondine which, scorning the haunts of commercial speculation, burst upon the world in 1935 as an out-and-out racing machine. It had a transverse four-cylinder engine, with the cylinders all sloping forward at 45 deg. from the vertical. Although they could well have been cooled by air and all have enjoyed an equal share of this undoubtedly cheap and lightweight coolant, the engine was in fact water-cooled. This was probably necessary because it was also supercharged, and, of course, boosted induction invariably brings as a corollary very high temperatures in certain localities such as the exhaust ports and sparking plugs, from which places heat can best be abducted by a liquid medium.

The engine of the Rondine was quite beautiful, with two overhead camshafts perched above its cylinder head, the timing mechanism occupying the central position between two adjacent pairs of cylinders. Ignition was by coil, and the clutch was a multi-disc affair running immersed in oil. The frame and forks were of pressed steel, beautifully contrived to give the utmost of rigidity with the minimum of weight, and other interesting details included an elongated seat which allowed the rider to assume a variety of positions according to the exigencies of whatever course he was negotiating. Readers accustomed to modern racing seats will scarcely find in this anything remarkable, but in the 1930s it was usual for a racing motorcycle to have a somewhat scanty saddle conventionally located, while on the rear mudguard was stuck a small and ill-shaped pillion seat to which the rider would transfer his long-suffering posterior whenever the opportunity to go really fast made it advisable for him to 'get down to it' and adopt a prone riding position. Thus the Rondine set yet another fashion; but it most deserves recollection as being the machine from which the famous and all-conquering Gilera was to evolve.

It must not be thought that the Rondine was an isolated example of burgeoning Italian art in the motorcycle sphere, for in that same year of 1935 there appeared the Azzariti, a vertical twin of 344 c.c. capacity, rejoicing in two overhead camshafts. Neither this machine nor the Rondine was to appear at the Isle of Man, but Italy was, to put it mildly, adequately represented there.

Long before the TT season got under way in 1935 there was an interesting motorcycle show at Berlin. Some of the machinery there was of particular interest, not least the

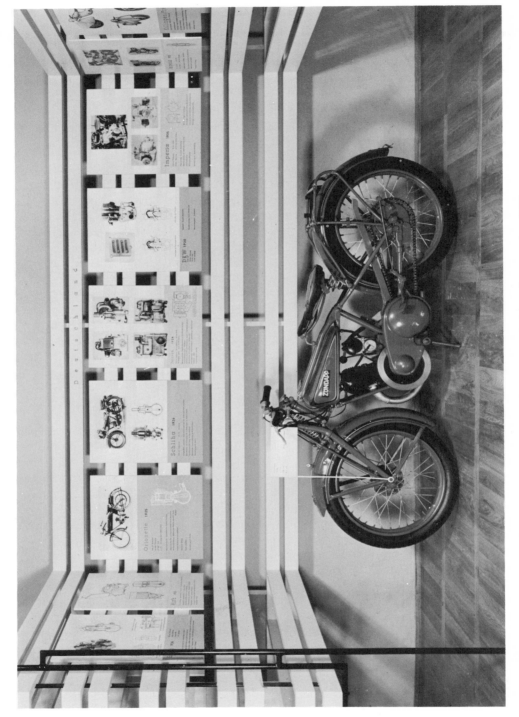

German Zündapp, typical of the workmanlike but technically uninspired Continental two-strokes (133)

500 c.c. Imperia. This was powered by a horizontally-opposed two-cylinder two-stroke, whose air-cooled cylinders were disposed athwart the frame and supplied with mixture from a supercharger. Even more remarkable was the fact that there was no gearbox: instead, a hydrokinetic torque converter was built on to the back of the crankshaft, and this was deemed to suffice, for from it a drive shaft led straight to the rear hub. The maximum speed claimed for this machine was 87 m.p.h., which was approximately what could be expected of a good super-sporting 500 c.c. single of conventional British manufacture, and therefore not to be decried in this German machine which carried quite full touring equipment.

Also at the Berlin show was a Zündapp whose major contribution to a quiet life was the use of chain in the gearbox, connecting sprockets on main and lay shafts rather than having the gears of these shafts meshing in the usual manner. On another stand could be seen the racing 250 DKW, now available as a production racer and to all intents and purposes the same as the works machine that had already proved very successful in competition. The basic engine formula was by now well established by DKW: a split-single water-cooled blown two-stroke with flat-topped pistons. In fact most German two-strokes had by now adopted the Schnuerle loop scavenge system. BMW had also something new to show, in the form of telescopic coil-sprung and oil-damped front forks on their machines, while NSU had some racing o.h.c. singles of 350 and 500 c.c. capacity.

In Germany, highly developed designs like these were not only acceptable but positively welcomed as evidence of the engineering competence and adventurousness of Nazism. Such things would not do in Britain or in America, where life was very difficult indeed. Many manufacturers of cars and motorcycles disappeared in the years immediately following the slump, and money became far too scarce for far too many people, with the result that motorcycles had, if they were to sell, to be cheap and therefore simple utilitarian things. There was neither room, nor money, nor inclination for anything exotic. Of course there remained a gilded nucleus, but they were fully occupied in stemming off the pursuits of eager vendors anxious that they should become the proud owners of some Bentley, Delage or Rolls-Royce; motorcycles were by and large for the masses, and the masses had no money.

Again there were exceptions. There were some men of sporting inclination and discernment who remained faithful to the motorcycle and who continued to demand the best; among them T. E. Lawrence, who was killed in a road accident while astride one of his beloved Brough Superiors on May 23, 1935. British riders, or British manufacturers, remained supreme in international motorcycling competition. The Canadian Alec Bennett we have already mentioned briefly as winning *inter alia* the Junior TT in 1926 on a Velocette. He repeated this victory in 1928, after winning the '27 Senior on a Norton, and he was tremendously successful on the Continent, notably in the Belgian and French Grands Prix. Then there was Walter Handley, the first man ever to win two TTs in one week, a feat that he performed in 1925. Handley started racing in 1922 at the age of 18, riding an OK-Blackburn in the Lightweight TT and promptly making the fastest lap at a speed 5 m.p.h. higher than had been achieved the previous year. For the five years from 1924 to 1928 he rode Rex-Acme machines, and put up a particularly brilliant display in the 1926 Senior TT when he finished second after suffering long delay through trouble in the second lap. In thirteen years of riding he rode in twenty-eight TTs of which he won four, finished second three times, twice third and made nine record or fastest laps. After 1934 he turned to car racing and was quite successful, although he never became as outstanding as certain other motorcyclists have done in the four-wheeled world. Motor-

1928 Austrian Grand Prix winner: Karl Gall, BMW (134)

Langman on Scott again, this time in the 1928 Senior (135)

The start of the 1928 Dutch Grand Prix. Graham Walker (60), W. Evans (51), Stanley Woods (45), Harry Perry (43) (136)

Charlie Dodson, winner of the 1928 Senior, on a Sunbeam (**137**)

cyclists seem in fact to make very good racing drivers, as witness the present exploits of John Surtees, and the earlier brilliant achievements of erstwhile racing motorcyclists such as Tazio Nuvolari and Bernd Rosemeyer.

There was another rider, Jimmy Simpson, who rode in twenty-six TT races and was almost invariably one of the fastest present, but who only won one race, the 1934 Lightweight, on a Rudge. Originally a trials and hillclimb rider, Simpson went on to win many international Grands Prix, and he had a long and successful career, first on AJS and then on Nortons, until his retirement in 1934. It was generally reckoned that any race in which he took part would be won by somebody else, but only after Simpson had led the field and probably established a new lap record. In fact he is distinguished for having been the first rider to have lapped the Isle of Man at 60 (in 1924), 70 (in 1926) and 80 m.p.h. (1931).

More successful, both in the Island and on the Continent, was Scotsman Jimmy Guthrie, who spent much of his long riding career on Nortons, championing them consistently from 1920 to 1937 apart from a year spent on AJS in 1930. The race for which he will probably be best remembered was the 1935 Senior, when he was generally thought to have won—only to be disillusioned, while receiving his plaudits, with the news that he had in fact lost by a mere four seconds. He came close to winning the German Grand Prix of 1937, too—but within a mile of the finish, while well in the lead, he crashed at the last corner and died shortly afterwards.

T. Spann's AJS for the 1929 Junior displays chain drive to overhead camshaft (**138**)

Rudge in 1930 Senior . . .

. . . and Jawa in 1932 Senior **(139–140)**

Finally, let us consider a Dubliner who won ten TT races, the earliest in 1923 and the last in 1939. This was Stanley Woods, who on a results basis must be recognized as the greatest of all Manx competitors. His first TT race was on a Cotton in the 1922 Junior, when he finished fifth despite a fire and chronic lack of brakes. He joined Norton in 1926, winning the Senior race of that year, the Senior and Junior of 1932 and 1933, but for some reason not doing quite so well in races on the Continent as did some of his British team mates. Woods changed to foreign machinery in 1934 when he rode the Swedish Husqvarna; in the year after that he piloted Guzzi machinery and was in fact the man who snatched from Jimmy Guthrie a four-second victory in the Senior TT, by dint of turning his last lap at the then astonishing speed of 86·5 m.p.h.

The foreign menace to British supremacy in motorcycling was stronger in 1935 than ever before. There was a threat from DKW who had a 500 c.c. machine there as well as a 250. Guzzi had the wide angle V-twin 500 there in the hands of Woods and Tenni; and in Senior practice there was also a menace in the form of a Jawa.

134

A Velocette makes a neat one-point landing at Ballig Bridge in 1933 (**141**)

Against this, it seemed that the most advanced thing the British could do was to fit alloy rims to the wheels of the TT Rudges. However, Guthrie won the Junior race on the Monday of TT week, which made the fifth time in a row that Norton had won this event. On the Friday there was the Lightweight race, won by Woods on the single-cylinder Guzzi, upon which he broke the lap record despite poor visibility. This was the first TT win by a spring-framed motorcycle, and the first win by a foreign machine since an Indian captured the Senior title in 1911. It was, incidentally, Woods' seventh TT win and augured well for the following day when the Senior race was contested over the same 264¼ miles. At first, as we have described, it was thought that Guthrie had won on his Norton, but Woods snatched back the lead by thrashing his Guzzi round the last lap at a speed more than 6 m.p.h. higher than his own fastest lap of the preceding year. He won by 4 seconds; and by this narrow margin was the foreign menace translated into hard, inescapable fact. Guzzi had issued the warning in 1926; and now it was Guzzi who in 1935 delivered an ultimatum that could not be met.

The mighty Cross-Rudge, spectacular entrant in the 1935 Senior. The massive cylinder head contained one of the few working examples of the Cross rotary valve. **(142)**

1936-1949
5 Sophistication

Progress, therefore, is not an accident,
but a necessity . . . It is a part of nature.
Herbert Spencer: *Social Statics*

After winning the 1936 Junior TT, Freddie Frith handed his Norton to a marshal and ran, actually *ran*, up the paddock. Such a display would have been unthinkable in earlier years because the spine-jarring ride of the rigid-frame motorcycles left the rider shattered and exhausted after completing the punishing Isle of Man course. But the Nortons for 1936 had spring frames, and this development not only improved the already outstanding steering and roadholding of the Norton, but also gave a more comfortable ride, as Frith so vividly demonstrated. The British Press went wild about the Nortons, conveniently forgetting that the eminently successful Guzzis of the previous year had also demonstrated the virtues of the spring-heel bicycle. Nevertheless, the 1936 series marked the beginning of an era in which fully-sprung motorcycles were to be widely developed; and this development made possible a sequence of technical advancements in other respects that was to continue unabated (save for an unavoidable hiatus while the Second World War was being fought out) right into the 1950s.

By the mid 1930s, motorcycles had already as much power as they could use. The new development of the spring frame, which we have shown was experimented with spasmodically from the earliest days of motorcycling but which had never received proper attention, now made it possible to keep both wheels of the motorcycle on the ground for a greater proportion of the total time. This improved adhesion made it possible to transmit more power to the back tyre, to employ more powerful braking, and thus to exploit increases in engine power which could continue to be obtained by known methods.

Common workaday motorcycles were not fully to reap the benefits of all this until well after the war, but a lot of necessary development work was done in the pre-war racers. Thus we find that the 1936 factory-entered Nortons not only had their plunger springing at the rear, but also a new composite cylinder barrel, with its iron liner cast into the alloy block, similarly composite construction of the cylinder head whose main bulk of light alloy encompassed a skull-type insert of aluminium bronze, and a two-spark magneto. Velocettes also turned up with spring frames, not the 'garden gate' plunger variety such as Norton employed, but a modern-looking trailing fork sprung by telescopic units in which compressed air provided the springing medium and oil the damping. The big square-finned cylinder head was of light alloy with inserted valve seats, and there was new twin-overhead-camshaft valve gear. The Vincent HRD, of course, had long made the most of a sprung rear wheel, and one of the ways it made the most of its superior adhesion was in very efficient braking, given by twin drums on each wheel—claimed to produce a symmetry of braking forces which avoided the distortion that might otherwise take place in the front forks. The DKW too had big brakes, disposed centrally in the wheel to produce much the same freedom from distortion. With all this improved road-worthiness, more power could be used; and it was remarked that compression ratios had climbed to new high levels, as much as 9:1 in the 500 c.c. singles, and $10\frac{1}{2}$:1 in the 250s.

Already the technological might of the major Continental teams such as DKW and BMW from Germany and Guzzi from Italy was making a continuation of the traditional British lead in motorcycle road racing somewhat difficult to guarantee. On paper the European machines were much more advanced and potentially winners every time. In practice they proved to lack the reliability of the old-fashioned but thoroughly developed British factory-entered motorcycles, which could not so easily be toppled from their traditional pinnacle in the Isle of Man and on the Continent.

Towards the end of the 1936 season the German lightweights proved to have the necessary stamina and began to clean up the 250 c.c. races, and the German and Italian firms, rejoicing in the patronage of their totalitarian masters, were the undoubted technological leaders. This made it all the more creditable that in 1936 350 and 500 Nortons won every big race but one. Nevertheless, by the end of the year the British riders were complaining that no unsupercharged single-cylinder machine could compare for speed and acceleration with the supercharged BMW. For that matter they said the unblown Guzzi was as fast as the BMW, and since they had good reason to expect it to appear the following year in supercharged form, they were feeling rather despondent. They could hardly rely on the advanced road-holding and steering of their new spring-framed machines, for by the end of 1936 both Guzzi and BMW were similarly sprung.

BMW were not content to strive for leadership only in the racing field. They also returned to the record-breaking arena in which they had been so active some years earlier. Back in 1930, and for some time afterwards, they had done wonders with a big 750 c.c. flat twin, partially faired to reduce wind resistance; but now they produced a new 500 completely enclosed in an egg-shaped aluminium shell with a tail fin. Ernst Henne raised the world speed record for motorcycles with this machine to a staggering 169·14 m.p.h. in October 1936. This run took place on the Frankfurt to Darmstadt Autobahn, after 6 a.m. practice on the more sinuous autobahn running from Munich to Landengränze. A week earlier the BMW team manager, Herr Sleischer, had said: 'We are finished with the 750 —the blown 500 is already giving much more power.' And so it was: there were rumours of unofficial clocking of the flying egg at something like 200 m.p.h. during practice runs.

At the actual record session, Britain's Eric Fernihough was there too, having been invited to come along with his famous supercharged Brough Superior. He opened proceedings by attacking and breaking Henne's old record for the standing kilometre, lifting it from 94·195 to 98·91 m.p.h. A strong wind was blowing down the course and in one direction Fernihough reached 113 m.p.h. Then Henne was pushed off to attack the flying kilometre record, his machine retracting its two little outrigger wheels as it got under way. Such was the wind that in one direction the BMW covered the measured kilometre at 180·197 m.p.h., but the average for the runs in each direction brought it down to a little over 169. Nevertheless, the new record was a clear 10 m.p.h. higher than the old one which Fernihough had been hoping to beat but now felt unable to attack with any hope of success.

Later in the year Fernihough took his Brough out to another fast road, this time at Gyon in Hungary. There he had a crack at Henne's old 1930 BMW record for the standing mile. Riding his 996 c.c. supercharged Brough with partial fairing, though terribly rudimentary compared with the complete streamlining of the BMW, he set a new record of 108·24 m.p.h. He took the flying mile, too, at a speed only a fraction under 170 m.p.h.

With the autumn of 1936 there came the motorcycle show at Earls Court, with an

1937 supercharged 500 BMW (143)

opportunity to evaluate British design. One could hardly draw any conclusions about the trends in any other country, for the only foreign machines present were BMW, Harley-Davidson and Indian. Nevertheless, it was in Britain that one of the most outstanding new designs was born.

This was the new Vincent HRD Rapide, a 1,000 c.c. V-twin that was to augment the existing range of 500 c.c. singles. In effect this new engine consisted of a pair of the existing HRD Meteor 500 singles mounted on a new common crankcase to make a compact V-twin of 47 deg. included angle. The cylinder barrels were light alloy, with nickel chrome liners. Good materials were evident in many places, such as the combined oil and fuel tank which was made of stainless steel. As in the earlier machines, there were duplex brakes on front and rear wheels, and indeed the whole motorcycle was, apart from the engine, little different from the existing 500s, weighing scarcely more than 410 lb. and being only $3\frac{1}{2}$ inches longer in its $58\frac{1}{2}$ inch wheelbase. This evidently fast and equally evidently well-made machine was marketed for £138, only £2 less than the ss100 which was the most expensive machine in the Brough Superior range.

Most other British machines followed time-honoured design. Some new trends were apparent, such as the adoption of constant voltage control, in, for example, the Nortons;

Schoolboy's dream, vintage 1938: Brough Superior 'Golden Dream'. George Brough's last fling had a coupled-crankshaft horizontally opposed 4-cylinder engine. Only four or five were made (144)

pressed steel frames in such as the Coventry Eagle; and a widespread adoption of complete valve gear enclosure and of rubber insulation for handlebars and petrol tanks, both of which were otherwise liable to suffer too much vibration from the usually rigid frame. Minor variations in detail there were in confusing abundance, rationalization being apparently unknown to the industry. Most firms offered several models, though they all followed the same basic theme of a moderately-tuned single-cylinder four-stroke in a rigid diamond-pattern frame with girder front forks, a saddle tank, and probably a foot-operated gear change. There was also a large number of essentially utilitarian two-strokes, the sporting two-stroke being a rare bird indeed. The Scott, of course, was a two-stroke and essentially sporting, but was always out of the ordinary and something of an acquired taste. An analysis of all the machines shows that $83 \cdot 7$ per cent of them had single-cylinder engines, a further $13 \cdot 4$ per cent being two-cylinder affairs. In the valve gear department, push-rod operated o.h.v. accounted for $58 \cdot 7$ per cent, while there were 17 per cent of side-valvers and $6 \cdot 3$ per cent with overhead camshafts. Two-strokes accounted for $17 \cdot 7$ per cent. In transmissions, $72 \cdot 9$ per cent were four speed and $21 \cdot 3$ per cent three speed, the remainder offering either according to choice and pocket; $64 \cdot 2$ per cent of these gearboxes had a foot-change mechanism, $27 \cdot 5$ per cent were hand operated, and a large number offered a choice. Twenty-six per cent of the machines on show had a larger-section rear tyre than at the front, a design feature that was due to become more and more common as the years went by. Finally, in the matter of ignition, $67 \cdot 2$ per cent had magneto, $17 \cdot 4$ per cent had coil. Some of the two-strokes had the simple flywheel magneto, such as had been developed by Villiers for the two-stroke engines that they supplied to so many manufacturers.

From these figures emerges a picture of an astonishingly standardized concept of motorcycle. No other major producing country in the world had so little variety. In France, for example, there were usually two or three four-cylinder machines, a number of shaft drives, several pressed-steel frames, and unit construction of engine and gearbox often apparent in the pricier machinery. There was always that nice flat-twin made by Gnome et Rhône, and the handsome high-camshaft Dax single, but economic depression tended to favour cheaper workaday machines, usually 500 c.c. singles. These were usually condemned to a miserable fate being slogged unmercifully at low speeds in top gear by peasants and artisans who treated their motorcycles in much the same way as they had long treated their cars, giving them little or no maintenance or consideration but expecting everything of them and gradually driving them into the ground.

Another feature of the French market was the large number of what they called 'velomoteurs'. These were usually 100 c.c. two-strokes, built to exploit regulations that allowed tax exemption to motorcycles weighing less than 30 kilogrammes. Similar regulations existed in several other European countries, and produced kindred machinery. Still, for the main range of the French market, it could be said that there was a distinct air of glamour about them, with lots of vivid colours and gay brightwork. France was still the undisputed top of the fashion world, and her elegance extended to her manufactures. Thus for those misguided enough to like side-cars, there were none like the French for elegance and beauty of line, just as the leading Parisian carrossiers were without peer in the creation of beautiful coachwork for exotic cars like the Delage, Delahaye and Hispano-Suiza.

Belgian machines were by contrast more mundane, the solid and straightforward FN and Sarolea being the best known.

For a combination of good sound engineering with technically advanced specification one would look to Germany. This country, rejoicing in the first and best of educational systems, had risen to be scientific leader of the world, and its new technocracy was showing its mettle in motorcycles as in everything else. There was more originality of design from German manufacturers in the late '30s than from any other source. To be sure, the German machines known best abroad (the racing BMW and DKW) were by no means typical of the domestic product. The production BMW had a fair amount in common with the racer, superficially at any rate—the transverse flat-twin engine and shaft drive being adhered to like a religious tenet. But the BMW was a costly machine and had an appropriately limited public, though it was also taken up in some quantities by the police, the army and other organizations of similarly official (not to say officious) nature. The DKW on sale to the public was far more mundane than the racer, a simple two-stroke distinguished only by the flat-top piston which, we have already seen, had become the outstanding DKW feature. There were a number of other two-strokes as well, many of them first class: sometimes they had exhaust ports facing to the rear of the machine, which allowed a straight exhaust pipe. This was popularly supposed to cause cooling difficulties, but in fact it has been pointed out in the past three years that better cooling of a finned cylinder is to be achieved by guiding the air from the cool or inlet side round to the hot or exhaust side than can be achieved by having the air flow in the opposite direction.

In Germany the two-stroke was the main plank of the utility market. All new motorcycles were tax free, and no driving test was necessary before riding a machine of less than 200 c.c. As a result, ultra-lightweight machines were extremely popular. Nevertheless the variety of design thinking in Germany led to a commendable variety of machinery. For example, there were a flat twin and a flat four in pressed-steel frames from Zundapp, and another flat twin from Victoria. Vertical single-cylinders were favoured by NSU, Ardie and Standard. NSU and several others featured unit construction of engine and gearbox. Good electrics were the rule, Germany being notably in advance of other countries in electrical engineering, and one of the ways in which this superiority was demonstrated was in the frequent fitment to German machines of dynamos of unusually high output.

Italy went about things in a different way, as might be expected from the more mercurial disposition of the national character. O.h.v. singles were the rule, frequently sporting, almost invariably smart, and more often than not spattered with bits and pieces appealing to the Italian's fondness for having a lot of taps to twiddle. Spring frames were common, probably because of the tendency of the Italians to run high-speed endurance tests on second-rate roads. There were many hot 175 c.c. four-strokes, even more 250s. The Rondine racer recorded in our last chapter as making its appearance was also produced in small numbers as a road-going machine, but it was only a sideline from a car manufacturer and was seldom to be seen on the road. Before long it was to be taken over by the Gilera firm who had already put up a very good showing in international trials with their side-valve models.

In Austria, German motorcycles were as common as might be expected, but British sporting singles were also popular. The most outstanding of domestic products was the two-stroke Püch, available either as a split-single or as a split-twin. Its neighbour, Czechoslovakia, produced mainly singles, with the leading firm of Jawa producing machines in all sizes. By contrast, two-cylinder machines were the vogue in Scandinavia, the best-known Swedish machine being the Husqvarna. Denmark produced the unusual four-cylinder Nimbus: this had an air-cooled in-line engine with overhead valves, and the

BMW broke through in the Isle of Man in 1939, winning the Senior at 89·38 m.p.h., a record that would stand for a decade. This is Georg Meier (**145**)

car-type transmission line of clutch, gearbox and final shaft drive was encompassed by an open cradle frame of pressed steel, a constructional method popular on the Continent because of its light weight and (given careful design) ample rigidity. In fact the Nimbus weighed a mere 380 lb., considerably less than many British machines of half the capacity and a quarter the number of cylinders.

Holland, the home of the Eysink, went in for single-cylinder motorcycles and noisy exhausts. Regulations similar to those in France and Germany encouraged a large number of ultra-light two-strokes.

Switzerland was a country in which regulations had abounded for generations, regulations covering practically everything. This bureaucratic safety-conscious and money-conscious nation was not entirely fond of motorcycling, although it produced its own Motosacoche which was very good. Super-sports British machines were surprisingly popular in Switzerland too, despite high import duties and very costly insurance.

America was distinguished from all these other countries in that singles were outnumbered by twins and fours of large capacity, anything from 750 to 1,400 c.c. The American motorcycle was huge, heavy and apparently terribly unwieldy, but had to be seen in its proper context. Travel in the USA at that time was a matter either of covering immense distances over good fast roads, or else of enduring very heavy going over poor, rutted, inadequately surfaced byways. The qualities developed in American motorcycles made them quite popular in some Continental countries and in a number of British colonies.

Such, then, was the pattern of motorcycling that was to endure until the end of the decade when the war was to call a halt to it all. This is not to say that nothing new was to emerge in those remaining years: George Brough, for example, felt the need for something different from the lusty and rakish V-twins he had been making so well for so many years, and came out with one or two short-lived oddities, such as the transverse-V-twin that made an appearance in 1937 and the transverse four-cylinder Golden Dream, with geared crankshafts, shaft drive and plunger rear springing, which appeared the following year and was made in minute quantities—probably only four or five. One or two other manufacturers also brought out new models, but usually they were merely the old ones modified in slight detail.

However, the racing fraternity could and would not content themselves with static design for long, and much more was to happen in the remaining three years of competition. Comparatively little of this was to be noted in 1937, which was a year of consolidation, marked by the increasing frequency with which DKWs appeared in the top placings of international lightweight races as their reliability improved, and by the turning of the first 90 m.p.h. lap of the Manx circuit in the Senior TT, when Freddie Frith rode a lap at 90·27 m.p.h. in the course of winning on his Norton. The results of the lightweight TT serve to remind us that the DKWs were not completely invincible, for that race was won by Omobono Tenni on a Guzzi, the best placed DKW finishing third behind Woods' Excelsior. In truth the Italian machines were proving very fast indeed, but the DKW was for a time almost unbeatable in the 250 class, although it never made the same impression in the larger classes. The 250 DKW had a water-cooled two-stroke engine of split-single design with a third supercharging cylinder, and was tremendously fast: it could outrun many 350s of the time. It was also remarkable for its dipsomaniac thirst, being capable of only about 15 m.p.g. at racing speeds, and for an ear-splitting exhaust note that could be heard at a range of several miles.

The pace of development quickened considerably in 1938. The TT results were not

144

altogether typical of the year's racing, save that the placed machines in all races were rear-sprung. This was new to the Excelsior and also to AJS, who that year produced a V-4 with one pair of cylinders sloping forward and the other back, in an effort to bring to bear sufficient sheer power to rival the foreigners. The other notable thing about the TT results in 1938 is that Norton's long run of successes in the Junior event (they won seven in a row) was stopped by Velocette.

The 1938 Nortons were quite new in many respects. The engine was redesigned to have greater bore and shorter stroke, so that it could turn faster; the result was a power output of about 48 b.h.p. and a speed of 6,500 r.p.m. on 80 octane fuel. The following year the Norton was to be the first unsupercharged engine to attain the magic figure of 100 b.h.p. per litre, a distinction that it was long to enjoy.

More apparent than these engine changes, however, were Norton's new telescopic front forks. These were set at a more shallow angle than the steering axis, and had springs for bump and for rebound but no damping. BMW appeared with telescopic forks, too, but in their case hydraulic damping was incorporated, though there were no rebound springs.

Possibly the most important racing machine to make its appearance in 1938 was the Gilera. This was a direct derivative of the four-cylinder Rondine design by Giannini, the Moto Gilera motorcycle firm (which began its history in 1909) having taken it over from the car firm. Supercharged, water-cooled, with its cylinders almost horizontal in a tubular double-cradle frame suspended at the rear by trailing forks and at the front by girder forks of pressed-steel construction, the Gilera was the first really successful example of the high-performance four-cylinder motorcycle. Although terribly complicated and costly to make, the four-cylinder engine with its smooth torque, low transmission loadings resulting from its even delivery of power impulses, and high potential power due to the relatively great piston and valve area and high rotational speeds made possible by the short stroke, had everything to recommend it. In 1938 the Gilera did very little racing, but it made its mark nevertheless, covering more than 121 miles in one hour in a convincing demonstration of performance and reliability.

The following year international motorcycle competition was in a real foment. The British riders of works Nortons and Velocettes tried all they knew with their traditional tested machinery; the works AJS team battled as well as it could in the face of mechanical unreliability and the discomfiting air of confidence about in the Continental teams. For the first time the European 500 c.c. championship went to Gilera.

The Italian firm, so new to racing, did not enter for the 1939 TT. Italy was nevertheless well represented, especially in the lightweight class which was won by Ted Mellors on a Benelli. This was an unsupercharged machine, a single-cylinder affair with twin overhead camshafts, capable of turning at over 9,000 r.p.m. The valve gear was supported on beautiful light alloy lattice work.

In fact the Benelli was by no means the fastest 250 in the race, the DKW probably being capable of beating it over a moderate distance. Hitherto the Achilles heel of the German two-stroke had been spark plugs, which suffered terribly from overheating—as might be expected in a supercharged two-stroke, which is just about the worst thing that can happen to a spark plug. However, this problem had been overcome, only the prodigious fuel consumption of the DKW holding it back by forcing it to make more refuelling stops than might be needed by some of its more frugal competitors. Faster than either the Benelli or the DKW was the Guzzi, which now appeared in supercharged form: supercharging a single-cylinder four-stroke is not easy, but the Guzzi people had overcome most of the problems by interposing a large chamber between the blower and the cylinder, which served to dampen the pulsations emanating from the single inlet port, at the cost of delayed throttle response. Of the English machines, the only one to figure was the Excelsior which finished third in the hands of Tyrell-Smith and rejoiced in new connecting rods of RR56 hiduminium alloy which ran direct on a nitralloy crank pin without any other bearing material intervening. The Excelsior was a mile an hour slower than the DKW of Kluge who finished second, and he in turn was more than $1\frac{1}{4}$ miles per hour slower than Mellors who won at 74·25 m.p.h., while the fastest lap was turned by Woods on the blown Guzzi at 78·16. The Junior class was still a British benefit, Velocettes winning with a Norton coming second ahead of a DKW. There was also a challenge from NSU, who fielded a supercharged 360 deg. twin, whose two cylinders were inclined forward at about 45 deg. and carried twin overhead camshafts. The NSU also had a vast fuel tank to cater for its terribly heavy fuel consumption.

In the 500 c.c. class most starters resembled the 1938 models, with the exception of the V-4 AJS which was now water-cooled because of the overheating problems caused by its being supercharged. Velocette turned up with a completely new racer and ran it a little during practice, but it did not race. More is the pity, for it has never been able to race since, being essentially a supercharged design. Nicknamed 'the Roarer', it had two vertical cylinders parallel to each other and connected by geared crankshafts to give well-nigh perfect balance. Alongside the gearbox was a Centric supercharger, and the final drive was by shaft. However, another supercharged two-cylinder shaft-drive machine was to win, and very convincingly: the BMW of Georg Meier won at a new record speed of 89·38 m.p.h., and was backed up by another BMW ridden by Jock West who finished second; the best that Norton could do was finish third. It was a very creditable best bearing in mind the fundamental antiquity of the design and the tremendous handicap of being atmospherically inspired rather than having forced induction. One must nevertheless face the fact that the regulations allowed superchargers, and anybody who had any sense would make the most of the regulations.

A detailed examination of the 1939 TT field reveals some interesting facts and comparisons. Unit construction of engine and gearbox was surprisingly common, being a feature of the BMW, of the Velocette twin, and of the 250 and 500 Guzzis, as well as of NSU, Benelli and Excelsior. The weights of the various machines also tell us a lot, and there are some surprises here: portly though it looked, the BMW was in fact the lightest of the 500s, the works machine turning the scales at a mere 306 pounds, while the standard over-the-counter BMW weighed 351 pounds. The British 500s were all in the region of 330 pounds, the 350s being only 15 pounds lighter. The 250 Benelli was surprisingly heavy, perhaps, at 293 pounds, compared with the 238 of the Rudge in the same class. Both of these, nevertheless, were appreciably lighter than the 250 DKW which weighed 320 pounds, 16 pounds less than its 350 c.c. stablemate. We have already recorded the vast fuel tank of the 350 NSU, which enabled it to carry some 50 pounds of fuel; this in addition to the machine's nett 369 lb weight made it one of the heaviest motorcycles running, but the V-4 AJS also had a prodigal thirst, and fuel tankage to match, and its basic weight was 405 pounds—small wonder that it could hardly compete with the BMW. One of the most interesting facts to emerge from this study is that the weight of the winning 500 c.c. machine was almost exactly the same as that of the 500 winner in 1929 (Dobson's longstroke Sunbeam), but the BMW was 25 per cent faster. It is a pity that ordinary production road-going motorcycles did not afford the same sort of comparisons: by 1939 the average British 500 c.c. single weighed something

1939 AJS—water-cooled, supercharged, four-cylindered, and much too heavy (**146**)

like 400 pounds, which was twice as much as its equivalent of twenty years earlier.

So much then for the racing of 1939, and so much too for motorcycle development. Both were brought to a halt by the war, over which we will draw a veil since it did nothing to further the development of the motorcycle. To be sure, motorcycles were in use a great deal, and many a rider was killed. Often it happened far from the front line, a large number of casualties being suffered by motorcyclists escorting long and badly spaced army convoys.

But we will not dismiss the war without relating just one rather appealing story, which is set in Normandy a short while after the Allied invasion of France in 1944. The battleship HMS *Rodney* stood off the French shore during and after the Normandy landings, providing the sort of bombardment that with its nine 16-inch guns it was singularly well equipped to deliver. The bombardment had been eased, and after a time only one of the guns was active, lobbing 16-inch bricks inland with apparently monotonous regularity under the guidance of a small spotter aircraft which, after every bang, would radio back the instruction: 'Up a thousand.' Then there would come another bang, and again: 'Up a thousand.' This went on for a while until it occurred to somebody in the *Rodney* to enquire what was going on—when it transpired that the line of craters stretching progressively further inland was tracing the course of a solitary and no doubt very frightened German dispatch rider, who must have been wishing that he were astride a full-blown Rennsport BMW, instead of the lowly standard Wehrmacht-issue machine he was riding!

147

The motorcycle at war in North Africa—as carefully posed for the Ministry of Information (**147**)

When the war came to an end in 1945, motorcycle manufacturers did not merely pick up where they left off in 1939. In many respects their new machinery was no different from what they had then been making, but the industry as a whole had learned a great deal in the meanwhile, especially from the tremendous progress that had been made in aero engine design and manufacture. In the case of some manufacturers of sufficient resilience this technical progress was reflected in several post-war designs—the Vincent HRD, the Douglas and the Sunbeam, all of which made their appearance within a year of the war's ending.

In general, however, crippling financial problems at national and international level made all kinds of engineering production fraught with terrible difficulties. Progress in design and development was desperately hindered, and some materials were in such short supply that they could not be made available for anything so apparently mundane and unimportant as motorcycles. The world shortage of petrol made things no easier. Motorcycling suffered greatly as a result of all these manifestations of universal shortage. Especially in Great Britain motorcycling could for most people only be indulged in on the most economical footing. A sharp rise in prices made the situation even worse, and all these factors were responsible for a rash of new small low-powered two-wheelers of a type that hardly merited the word motorcycle.

Before we go on to read the depressing chronicles of the years of the moped and ultra lightweight, let us look at the splendid new models already named. In December 1945 the new Vincent HRD Rapide was announced, and Setright recalls seeing it on show in a motorcyle dealer's at Southend, one of the many places in the country to which the machine was taken. Although the new Vincent HRD had something in common with the pre-war design, it was externally a lot cleaner. Known as the Series B, to distinguish it from its predecessor, it had a new engine which was designed to possess the utmost rigidity—an important feature since it not only provided the motive power but also constituted the centre portion of the frame. The ideals at which the Vincent HRD design team, headed by Phil Irving, had aimed were really idealistic: they wanted handling comparable with that of a TT 500, the motorcycle had to be as light as possible, all exposed face joints had to be relieved of such loads as might cause oil leaks, there were to be no plated or enamelled bits and pieces liable to rust, and as far as possible all external plumbing and other odds, ends and excrescences were to be avoided. In addition to all this the riding position had to be fully adjustable so as to be commensurate with the tremendous range of performance promised by the new machine.

All this was in some measure achieved. The beautifully made and finished V-twin engine, with its high camshafts, short pushrods and unusual rockers which engaged the valve stems half-way down (beneath the valve springs), generated 45 b.h.p. and had sufficient torque at its command to enable very high gear ratios to be pulled, so that at 80 m.p.h. the engine revs in top gear were only about 3,600. The speed possible with this power and this gearing was in the region of 112 m.p.h. and the acceleration was such as no previous road machine had ever offered. Even in top gear, a tweak of the throttle would send the machine leaping forward in acceleration that could really be felt from speeds as high as 70 or 80 m.p.h. Braking was equally good, the twin drums on each wheel giving stopping distances of a mere 20-odd feet from 30 m.p.h., considerably better than 1g. The handlebars were narrow and nearly straight, and contributed to the characteristic Vincent riding position, the rider's body being leaned forward at about 40 deg. from the vertical, while his feet were splayed out on wide-spaced footrests athwart the big gearbox and clutch. The clutch itself was interesting, being a centrifugally-assisted type such as might be found on some cars, with an auxiliary single-plate clutch for moving off from rest. Everywhere the detail was marvellous: tommy bars allowed really rapid wheel removal, there was a full range of adjustments for pedals, handlebars, gear lever, foot brake lever and just about everything else imaginable, the finish was superb, the noise level moderately low except for a certain amount of valve gear noise, and in every way the Vincent HRD 1000 promised to be a worthy successor to the late Brough Superior.

At about the same time, Douglas announced their new 350 c.c. flat twin. Unlike all previous Douglas twins except the short-lived Endeavour model of 1935, the engine was placed athwart the frame, and was a fairly high-efficiency pushrod four-stroke with wet sump lubrication. Behind it a car-type clutch linked the engine to a gearbox bolted up in unit with the crankcase, containing four speeds plus a pair of bevel gears which brought the drive out to a sprocket for the final chain drive to the rear wheel. The same cross shaft upon which this sprocket was mounted was also utilized to make possible a convenient kick-starter.

More remarkable than the engine was the frame of the new Douglas. Sturdy in itself, with its duplex cradle lay-out, it was most outstanding by virtue of the quite revolutionary suspension system that the Kingswood designers had devised. The front forks were bottom-link types, the legs or stanchions being very fat and tremendously stiff, and enclosing long helical springs compressed by the action of the short leading links mounted at the bottom of the stanchions to carry the wheel. At the bottom of each fork leg was a chamber containing oil and a valving system to provide damping for the spring. Wheel movement was considerable, and the springing soft, while the short links caused the wheels to describe an arcuate path that ensured a sensibly constant wheelbase for initial wheel movements around the static deflection point, and a sensibly constant trail during more violent compression of the springs. The back plate of the brake was fully floating and separately anchored to the front forks by a radius arm which ran parallel to the suspension links, so that the suspension was not inhibited by braking forces. At the rear, the suspension was equally unorthodox: the wheel was carried in a tremendously stiff trailing fork of welded box section, but springs and dampers were nowhere to be seen! Instead the fork legs were linked to cranks which were splined on to the rear ends of long torsion bars that passed through the bottom run of the frame and were anchored at the front end. The result was a stupendously good ride, combining remarkable comfort with extremely good steering and road holding. The Douglas demonstrators used to show off the bicycle's capabilities by riding on and off a 4-inch kerb three or four times at 30 m.p.h. without coming to grief—as they certainly would have done on any of the more rudimentary designs that were common.

Then in March 1946 there appeared the 500 c.c. Sunbeam. This was designed by Erling Poppe, son of the man who lent his name to the White & Poppe car of earlier years. Erling had been interested in motorcycles since his youth: he designed, built and rode some ferocious big twins in the 1920s, then went into the world of diesel engines and heavy vehicles, making himself quite a reputation there. Now he was back with motorcycles again and produced something quite outstanding in its modernity and lack of subservience to convention. The frame itself was not particularly remarkable, a duplex tubular structure incorporating plunger rear springing; but everything else was most unusual. The engine was an outstandingly beautiful creation, an in-line air-cooled monobloc two-cylinder design with a deep car-type sump beneath its crankcase. The bore was 70 mm., the stroke only $63 \cdot 5$, forecasting accurately the trend to short-stroke engines. (The Vincent and the Douglas were both virtually square, the latter for example having bore and stroke dimensions of $60 \cdot 8 \times 60$ mm.) The crankshaft was a casting, but fully balanced; the inevitable imbalance of the whole engine was accommodated by mounting it in rubber in the frame. This was almost unheard of in motorcycles, but must have gone a long way to improving comfort and frame durability. The elegantly and liberally finned main block of the engine was surmounted by a cylinder head cast in Y alloy and containing combustion chambers shaped to give squish as the pistons approached top dead centre; this improved combustion by increasing turbulence in the compressed mixture, enabling the most to be gained from each charge of the poor fuel available at the time. In fact British fuel was then so poor that the compression ratio was limited to 7:1, although an 8:1 sports version was to be produced later. The valves were in-line, and were operated by an overhead camshaft. The engine developed a modest (though not shameful) 25 b.h.p., but did so with a sweetness, smoothness and flexibility that belied any impressions of sporting intransigence that the idea of an overhead camshaft might have conveyed. It could never be a really high-performance engine, for its rear cylinder was starved of cooling air, and the attractive experimental 2-o.h.c. head designed for it would have needed redesign of the block to justify it.

As with the Douglas, the Sunbeam engine had a car-type clutch and close-ratio gearbox bolted up in unit behind it. Unlike the Douglas, though, Sunbeam opted for the shaft drive to which the layout so readily lent itself, and this was achieved with the aid of a nicely made worm-drive rear hub. This hub looked somewhat massive, but was dwarfed by the huge wheels and tyres that made the Sunbeam look quite unlike any other two-wheeler. The tyres were of 4·75—16 section, and the wheels were quickly detachable. Despite the air of massiveness lent by these huge tyres and the inevitably vast domed mudguards to cover them, the whole machine weighed only 390 pounds, which was not at all bad. Nevertheless there was no skimping in the design: the front forks, for example, were particularly sturdy and were free from the slackness and tendency to asymmetric loading which have always been the bugbear of conventional telescopic forks. In the Sunbeam, the fork stanchions were merely guides, and contained no springs. Instead, the spring was a single compression affair housed in a central tube, connected to the legs by a stirrup.

Everybody who tried the Sunbeam was loud in its praises, surprised by the excellence of its steering despite the corpulent tyres, and delighted by the top gear flexibility that embraced a range of speeds from 11 to 77 m.p.h.

Apart from these three distinguished machines very little that was new or good was to appear for some time. Most manufacturers were content to revive their pre-war models, tarting them up with new colour schemes and as like as not telescopic front forks, but doing very little else to indicate the passage of six or seven years.

The first motorcycle show to be put on after the war was in October 1946 at Paris. It was a brave effort, done for reasons more patriotic than commercial. All the exhibits there were somewhat notional, being invariably accompanied by a notice saying 'Not for Sale', 'Export Only', 'Price Unknown', and so on. France indeed was in a shocking mess, and certainly not in a position to entertain a vast market for luscious motorcycles. The mainstay of the French market was the *velomoteur*, which had been developed in the late 1930s, when the majority of these motorized bicycles were of sizes round about 50 c.c.; but now the authorities sanctioned the same dispensations as to tax, insurance, and so forth for all machines up to 125 c.c., so engine sizes increased. There was a surprising consensus of opinion among the designers of this myriad of two-wheeler runabouts: the cylinder barrels were invariably of light alloy, usually carrying liners of austenitic or martensitic iron with as like as not a coefficient of thermal expansion similar to that of the light alloy encompassing them. The finning of these cylinders was often contrived to give them an oval teardrop shape, and this styling of the exterior was augmented in most new models by a tendency to have the gearbox *en bloc* with the crankcase. Rear springing was popular, usually by plungers, and springing of the saddle virtually universal, so that even if the sprung frame was there only for looks, the Frenchman's carefully nurtured *dérrière* (have you noticed how the seats of French cars are much softer than those of any others?) was still protected by the amply sprung saddle.

As 1946 wore on, sundry other developments were noted as being on their way for the following year. Triumph, for example, announced that their future models would have as an optional extra a new design of internally sprung rear hub, which promised to give the lowest possible unsprung weight at the rear. It was a splendid idea, marred only by the impossibility of making the guides sufficiently durable while keeping them necessarily small, so that sloppiness and inaccurate running of the wheel proved eventually to be its undoing. Nevertheless the sprung hub had an excellent introduction to the motorcycling world when Ernest Lyons rode a special Grand Prix version of the 500 c.c.

151

Triumph Speed Twin to victory in the 1946 Manx Grand Prix, a race that was run in streaming rain when good rear wheel adhesion was at a premium.

Another announcement was of a new vertical twin from BSA, a 500 c.c. pushrod job left over from the 1939 development programme. Following the success of the 1935 Triumph, the vertical twin was clearly catching on in a very big way. Within the space of a year or two, every major British manufacturer was producing at least one engine of this type.

The recipe was always the same: a crankcase, set with the crankshaft athwart the frame as in a conventional single-cylinder machine, carried a crankshaft with both crankpins moving together, that is to say separated by 360 deg., so that the engine fired once every revolution but was no better balanced than a conventional single-cylinder engine. The cylinder barrels of cast iron carried detachable heads with hemispherical combustion chambers, the valves in which were operated by rockers and pushrods from a camshaft or camshafts somewhere down in the crankcase. Behind the cylinder head was usually a single Amal carburettor, while the exhaust ports faced forwards and slightly outwards so that the twin pipes could emerge into a free-flowing airstream and be swept sharply down before being carried to the rear where they discharged into silencers of moderate size. This engine invariably went into a frame that was basically a diamond shape but which might be endowed with some form of rear springing in the form of plungers or (in the case of Ariels) short trailing links, while the front forks were invariably softly-sprung telescopic types. Machines of this nature were frequently quieter than the equivalent single, invariably smoother, often not a little faster. In the majority of cases the differences were somewhat academic since the machines were not available on the home market and the overseas buyers were not particularly interested in the single-cylinder alternatives.

But if this was the way that the British industry was going, Continental Europe took quite a different view of things. In December 1946 eighteen Italian makers showed their wares at Milan, in company with Ariel who were the only foreign firm there. With that proper conception of the importance of racing machinery in relation to ordinary every-day road-going types, the Italians showed the Gilera 4 and a new racing Guzzi. The former was the machine as raced by Nello Pagani to win the 1946 Italian Championship: it was not dissimilar from the pre-war machine except that it was unsupercharged. However, a new one was promised for the following year, to be air-cooled and not water-cooled, the cylinders to be less sloped towards the horizontal, the engine to be given wet sump lubrication. There was also promise of improvement to the locally successful Gilera Saturno single-cylinder 500 c.c. racer.

Guzzi showed a new single-cylinder 500 racer christened the Gambalunga, literally 'long leg'. Designed to take advantage of a new national racing formula, the Guzzi was a brilliant piece of design, featuring trailing fork rear suspension, bottom link front suspension not unlike that of the Douglas but with longer links angled so as to give more or less constant trail over the major working portion of the front wheel's travel, big brakes and, most astonishing of all, a total weight of only about 180 pounds.

Apart from these unashamed racers, there were lots of sporting-looking machines intended for road use. Popular capacities were 500, 250 and 175 c.c.; there was not a single 350 in the show. All the Italian machines had rear springing, and two of them were noticeable as being excellent miniature copies of existing machines. One, a new make, was the Parilla, which turned out to be a super-sporting 250 looking for all the world like a miniature International Norton; then there was the Aspi 125, which was a boy's version of the BMW twin.

152

Like the French, the Italians were very conscious of the need to develop utilitarian and very cheap motorcycles. Lament it though one may, since the movement that it led to was partly responsible for the near strangulation of motorcycling, one must note the presence at this Milan show of the Vespa scooter. There were also no fewer than seventeen different types of auxiliary motors for powering pedal cycles, the most outstanding being the 48 c.c. Cucciolo which was unlike most of the others in being a pushrod four-stroke with two-speed gear, its complexities being justified by an output of $1\frac{1}{2}$ b.h.p. at 5,300 rev/min from a total weight of $17\frac{1}{2}$ pounds.

Vertical twins continued to come thick and fast. In March 1947 there was a new one from France, the 349 c.c. o.h.v. Sublime. This was a cobby, solid, good-looking job, plunger-sprung at the rear, telescopic forked at the front and with interchangeable wheels. But it did not last long.

There were quite a number of things that did not last long, coming on to the market in a brief experimental flurry and quietly dying a little later. For example, the sensation of the Geneva show in March 1947 was the new utility Motosacoche. This was a 200 c.c. side-valve affair with belt drive, a hand starter, and a transmission that exploited an expanding pulley whose dimensions were controlled hydraulically by high-pressure oil delivered from an engine-driven pump. Amongst the many oddities was a brakeless front wheel, the designer, Douglas (otherwise known as Dougal) Marchant, feeling that the sort of people for whom the machine was intended could not be trusted with a front brake. During the war Marchant had devised a fuel metering device that made a conventional carburettor unnecessary, so of course the Motosacoche had no carburettor either.

When everybody had finished raving about this new cheap runabout for the apparently teeming Swiss masses, they found time to look at some other designs including the handsome Swiss 500 c.c. flat twin Universal, the 580 c.c. side-valve flat twin Condor (another Swiss design that was and probably still is popular with the Swiss police), and, if they felt like looking at another flat twin of more advanced specification, they could always go along to the Douglas stand where the British 350 was to be seen. As in Paris and Milan, there were also lots of auxiliaries and sub-miniature motorcycles, all testifying to the universal need for cheap transport.

Another three months and it was TT time, the first TT since 1939. Superchargers were barred, fuel was limited to a ghastly 72 octane brew that was virtually indistinguishable from the Pool petrol that sullied roadside pumps throughout Great Britain, and there were widespread stories of difficulties arising from this noxious fluid. In fact it proved to put performance back by five years, best speeds being comparable with what had been achieved in 1935. There was no new machinery there except for two AJS Porcupines: neither of these got anywhere, one suffering from severe clutch slip in the first lap, the other ridden by a man with a badly injured left hand. It was an interesting machine nevertheless, with two parallel cylinders set very low down and horizontal in a duplex cradle frame with telescopic forks at the front and trailing forks at the rear. The nickname followed from the spike-type finning of the cylinder head in order to dissipate heat through the maximum surface to the cooling air, and the engine was surmounted and nearly smothered by a vast fuel tank shaped so as to provide some protection for the rider. Unfortunately the engine had been designed before the war to be supercharged, and it was impossible to achieve a satisfactory combustion chamber shape and at the same time raise the compression ratio to the level appropriate to an unsupercharged racer. This hampered the machine's performance severely, but not so much as the

153

terribly bad luck they had always suffered in the Isle of Man. Another design intended for supercharging was the 250 c.c. Guzzi, which nevertheless contrived in unsupercharged form to win and come second in the Lightweight TT.

By the end of 1947 a number of new things had been announced for the following year, most of them being known about before the Milan show in December, which featured lots of 125s. Prices there were still high because of labour difficulties in Italy, where imports were nil and exports negligible. In Britain these things were ordered somewhat better, and so we saw some interesting technical developments. One was the adoption of Dowty oleopneumatic forks, working in similar fashion to the rear suspensions struts on the pre-war racing Velocettes, on new machines by Panther, Velocette and EMC. These last were the brainchild of Erlich, 350 c.c. split-single two-strokes distinguished by the small number of fins (only four) on the cylinder, and having a remarkably lively performance.

The year 1948 saw the introduction in February of a limited number of Triumph Grand Prix racing machines that were to be made available to the privateers of the racing world if they could afford £343 for the privilege. The GP Triumph was in effect a replica of the bicycle on which Lyons won the Manx Grand Prix in 1946, although some development work had been done since. Many of the components of this 310-pound racer were lifted straight from the production Tiger 100 roadburner, but the engine, which was safe up to 7,600 rev/min, was rather special, owing its cylinder head to an engine developed by Triumph during the war as an aircraft auxiliary.

Shortly afterwards there came news of another big Vincent HRD twin, a super-sporting version of the Rapide that was already the world's fastest road-going motorcycle. Christened the Black Shadow, the new Vincent was immediately recognizable by the all-black finish applied to the exterior of the engine, cylinder barrels and heads, crankcase, brakes and all. As well as being an interesting bit of styling, the black finish did a useful job in improving heat dissipation and was done properly, as indeed most things were on these costly big twins: it was not just a matter of squirting black paint on to aluminium and letting it lift off later as in such circumstances it undoubtedly would—instead, the light alloy parts were all given a chemical treatment known as Pylumin, which guaranteed an excellent bond for subsequent paintwork. Beneath this Stygian exterior lurked higher-compression pistons, highly polished ports, rockers and connecting rods, and modified valve gear allowing the engine to make the most of larger bore carburettors. Ribbed cast-iron brake drums replaced the steel version on the tourer, and there were some differences in electrics and instrumentation.

The Black Shadow proved to be without peer on the road. *Motor Cycling* reported on it in July 1948, saying that it was impossible to state a definite cruising speed on the open road, the margin being set only by road conditions and rider's capabilities. Since the top gear maximum was found by them to be 122 m.p.h. (a French magazine managed 128), with acceleration over the standing quarter mile requiring less than 15 seconds and resulting in 92 m.p.h., the point was readily taken. The Vincent also proved to be a prodigious stopper, needing but $22\frac{1}{2}$ feet to come to a halt from 30 m.p.h. All the exclusive features and niceties of the touring Rapide, such as the comprehensive equipment, the fully adjustable controls and the high standard of finish, were still there, helping to justify a price on the British market of £381.

With the scarcely noted demise of the Zenith soon to follow, the Vincent HRD remained the only British big twin in production. The only other V-twins were being made in the USA, as they had been for so many years. This made it all the more interesting

Post-war extravagance in austere Britain. This is the 1948 four-cylinder Wooler 500 with prototype rocking-beam engine (148)

155

that at the 1948 Brussels show Harley-Davidson should introduce a little 125 c.c. two-stroke.

More significant was the Geneva Show in March 1948, at which the German makers staged a comeback of no mean order. Germany's industry was limited (by the terms of the nation's submission to the allied conquerors) to making motorcycles of not more than 250 c.c. capacity. This being so, it was scarcely surprising that most of the new machines were two-strokes: makers returning to the field included Ardie, NSU, Victoria and Zundapp. BMW were there too, with a 250 single with a frame that was clearly scaled down from the big twin, and had the same sort of transmission: the engine was virtually half a big twin stuck on end to look like a conventional pushrod single.

If the revived German industry was attracting a lot of attention at the Geneva Show, there were a lot of questions being asked about the revolutionary Swiss product that had made such an impact the year before. Where, everybody was asking, was the Motor-acoche? The momentous decision had been taken to abandon motorcycle manufacture after fifty years of producing some of the world's finest and best made motorcycles, not to mention all the engines provided by them (and bearing the initials MAG) for a host of other firms including Brough Superior, Matchless, Rex-Acme, and Lea Francis.

Three months after the Geneva show, Indian showed that Harley-Davidson were not the only American firm to be influenced by European trends. They announced two new models, both of which showed considerable British influence. The larger, reviving the famous old Scout name, was an o.h.v. vertical twin of 435 c.c., with a plunger sprung frame and a general air of Birmingham about it. There was also a rigid frame 217 c.c. single.

Such machinery was not altogether expected in Europe, and the curious engine capacities did nothing to enhance the Indian's popularity. But, if the Indian twin was not eagerly anticipated, there were thousands looking forward to the appearance of the new racing Gilera 4 from Italy. Its coming had been bruited about for some time, and many hopes were entertained of its being entered for the Isle of Man TT. Alas, the 257-pound Gilera was not ready for the Island; its first entry was for the Dutch TT

Without the Gilera challenge, the Senior TT became a fairly straightforward Norton benefit. More significant was the début in the Junior event of the 7R AJS. This had an entirely new engine, although based on the chain-drive overhead camshaft racing AJS that had originated in the 1920s. As is so often the case with a new racing machine due for a long and distinguished career, the 7R AJS did not finish in the money that year, but it proved itself more than adequately rapid, one of them in fact lapping faster than all but three of the 500s.

Such a promising start for the new racer provided a welcome boost to the morale of the British at a time when their supremacy was threatened by the insurgence of a horde of highly sophisticated special-purpose Italian motorcycles. Everyone was waiting for the racing début of the new Gilera and speculating on both its immediate and long term prospects. They did not have to wait long: the promised entries for the Dutch TT materialized, and a strong team of Gileras was fielded to do battle not only with the works Nortons but also with the V-twin Guzzis. Both the Italian makes issued a strong challenge in the early stages of the race, which was run at a somewhat slower speed than in the previous year because of the torrential rain that swept the course. The Gilera spearhead was Masserini, who kept the untried new 4 hard on the heels of the redoubtable Artie Bell, who led the Norton team and indeed the race. Further back Nortons, Gileras and Guzzis were mixing it with a ferocity that had to be tempered by respect for

156

Bob Berry record-seeking horizontally on his Brough (**149**)

the slippery road; but Masserini had the bit between his teeth, and paid for his audacity by falling off during the third lap while tailing the flying Bell. The Englishman was never headed.

As was usual at the time, the Italians displayed a marked uninterest in the 350 class, which was, as usual, cleaned up by Velocette. There was no lightweight class, but instead an ultra-lightweight 125 race that was full of the indigenous Eysinks and Italian Morinis.

The remainder of the racing year was not without its highlights, probably the toughest race being the Ulster G P that in 1948 took its turn to enjoy the dignity of being the Grand Prix d'Europe. If the Dutch race had been wet, the Ulster one was run in a deluge with winds of gale force adding to the riders' burden. The meeting being on British soil, it was natural that there should be a 250 class, though the multitude of British entires were properly trounced by an Italian machine, a Guzzi ridden by Maurice Cann. Frith won the Junior event on his Velocette—one is tempted to say 'of course'—but the Senior race was by no means a foregone conclusion. The winner was Lorenzetti riding a two-cylinder Guzzi, but Lockett finished behind him on a Norton, with the late Les Graham third on the Porcupine A J s. There was no ultra-lightweight race, but this was not so sadly missed as was that splendid rider Omobono Tenni, who a little earlier had been killed during practice for the Swiss G P on the very fast and peculiarly difficult Bremgarten circuit at Berne. Tenni was aged 43 when he died, and had been consistently the fastest of the Guzzi riders. His death hammered home the perils of the racing man's way of life, a lesson that was administered with double severity on that fateful weekend when one of the greatest of racing drivers, Achille Varzi, was also killed.

The end of 1948 saw the usual premature rash of new models for the following year, the first being a brace of big Harley-Davidson twins announced in September. These had typical huge Harley engines of 61 and 74 cubic inch capacity, roughly equalling 1,000 and 1,200 c.c. respectively. More significant, however, was the adoption on both of telescopic front forks.

By 1949 this type of front suspension was almost *de rigueur*. Of the manufacturers who steadfastly set their faces against the type, most outstanding and original were Vincent H R D, who evolved a new type of forks for the new Series C range marketed for 1949. These were the Girdraulic forks, the name being coined because their geometry was essentially that of the traditional girder forks, although the springing and damping media were of the type associated with the new telescopic forks. The Girdraulics were quite distinctive, the old multi-tubular girder structure having given way to a pair of immensely stiff forged blades of high duty alloy, behind which a pair of telescoping tubes enclosed coil springs and hydraulic damping. The whole arrangement looked very handsome and far less spindly than most of the telescopic forks from other manufacturers—indeed the majority of telescopics at this time were miserably sloppy affairs given to binding and lozenging in a way that did navigational accuracy no good at all. There are some who consider even the adoption of the Girdraulics a retrograde step: Phil Heath, who today is a motorcycling journalist whose right hand has not lost its cunning with a twist grip, used to compete on series B Vincents (indeed he finished second in the newly introduced 1,000 c.c. Clubman's event in the Isle of Man in 1948), and he believes that the old Brampton girder fork was better for cornering than the Girdraulic. 'The latter may give you a more comfortable ride, but flicking over from one side to another was much easier with the old type; the Girdraulics seem far too heavy and unresponsive in this respect.'

There were some other novelties for 1949, including coil ignition for Scotts (accompanied by howls of anguish from diehard magneto-fanciers) and a handsome new all-alloy engine for the Ariel Square 4, which not only cut down its prodigious weight by a considerable margin but also made new provision for cooler exhausts. There was also a weird new flat four from Wooler, the same family whose Flying Banana has been recorded in an earlier chapter. The Flat 4 Wooler had most unusual multiple plunger suspension fore and aft, had its exhaust running through the bottom tubes of the duplex frame (an expedient that was soon abandoned) and carried superimposed on the line-ahead gearbox casing a tool box containing two spanners, which were all that was necessary to dismantle the entire machine. Another new motorcycle, replete with unorthodoxy at a time when the market was proving addicted to the orthodox, was the little L E Velocette which has since gone from strength to strength. In later years it was to be cleaned up somewhat, given an optional foot-operated gearchange, and be expanded to 192 c.c.; but when it made its appearance it was only 149 c.c. and was overtly utilitarian. The engine was a transverse flat-twin, driving through a car-type clutch and unit-construction gearbox to the rear hub through the medium of a shaft universally jointed to accommodate the action of the trailing fork rear suspension. The engine was a

Grand old man of British motorcycling, the late Graham Walker, tries out the post-war vertical twin Indian Scout (150)

1947 Harley in the Laconia 100-mile road race (**151**)

side-valve and was water-cooled to assist mechanical quietness. The LE promptly became known as the 'silent LE', which was why it proved so attractive to police forces.

Another new manifestation was the motor scooter, a device that we refuse to grace with the description motorcycle, and which therefore has no place in this work. But if we are not to describe these machines in all their dissatisfying and undeserved detail, we cannot afford to dismiss them without lamenting the tremendously significant part they were to play. The importance of the motor scooter movement in bringing about the denigration and ultimate decimation of motorcyclists is strictly a topic for the following chapter, but even in the late 1940s the rot had already set in. The appearance of the Vespa has already been related; in Britain the Brockhouse organization weighed in with a tiny scooter called the Corgi, which had a 98 c.c. two-stroke engine and precious little else. Since it was cheap, easily handled, and appeared neither to demand nor to deserve any care or attention, it was soon to be seen in surprising numbers, only to disappear a few years later through its inability to compete with the more glamorous and sophisticated machines of Continental origin.

Let us, however, return to the real motorcycles that appeared at the end of this decade. There were among them two general trends: one was towards the adoption of fully sprung frames, the other towards a multiplicity of cylinders. The Ariel Square 4 had already been given an unusual spring heel in which an ordinary-looking pair of vertical plungers merely contained the springing and damping media, while the wheel was actually located by a short compound linkage that was designed to maintain constant tension in the final drive chain. For 1949 this spring heel was made available as an optional extra for Ariel's smaller Red Hunter singles and their new vertical twin. Royal Enfield, too, devised a new frame and with it a trailing fork rear suspension. Indeed the trailing fork, sprung by coils surrounding a hydraulic damper, the whole enclosed in telescopic dust-excluding covers, promised to be the new standard rear end. Something of this sort was to be seen on the whole new range of motorcycles from the big AMC organization, which was an amalgam of Matchless and AJS. The new Springtwins, as they were often called, were not externally dissimilar from other vertical twin motorcycle engines; but within they enjoyed the dubious advantage of a third main bearing between the two crankshaft throws. So now, in addition to the multitude of European firms, nearly all the major British manufacturers listed one vertical twin or more—AMC, Triumph, BSA and Ariel. In this popular big class, only Norton remained; and sure enough along came a vertical twin Norton—the Dominator 7, a 500 c.c. pushrod twin in an agricultural-looking frame, but energetic enough to give 95 m.p.h. on the road and to handle at least as well as other touring and semi-sports Nortons. In fact the Norton of 1949 was probably still the best behaved British machine with the exception of the remarkable 350 c.c. flat-twin Douglas, some of whose outstanding specification and extraordinary handling properties we have already recited. For a 350 the Douglas was also surprisingly quick: *Motor Cycling* had road tested one in 1948 and found it the fastest 350 they had ever tested in road-going form. The maximum speed was 78 m.p.h., with 25, 52 and 69 available in the indirect gears. The standing quarter-mile occupied about 20 seconds and at its end the speed was 69 m.p.h. Braking from 30 m.p.h. to a standstill needed but $31\frac{1}{2}$ feet. In 1949 the Douglas had reached its Mark III version, and it began to appear in the entry lists for Clubman's races.

Probably the most consistently outstanding machine in 1949 racing was Velocette, whose entries, directly and indirectly, enjoyed tremendous success in the 350 c.c. class. The most notable rider was Freddie Frith, who stands out as the one man who played a leading part in racing throughout the period covered by this chapter. Schooled in the Manx Grand Prix, Frith joined the Norton team in 1936 and justified the confidence of his entrants by promptly winning the Junior TT and finishing third in the Senior. In the following year he became the first rider to lap the TT course at over 90 m.p.h. His racing career continued after the war on Velocettes and occasionally Triumph or Guzzi machinery. 1948 was a year in which he gained many wins for Velocette; 1949 saw him so consistently the winner of the 350 class that he not only netted the world 350 championship but also, after his retirement at the end of the season, had the distinction of being the first motorcyclist to be given recognition in the honours list, being awarded the OBE for the good work he had done in maintaining British prestige.

While we are on the subject of famous riders we might just note that the Senior Manx Grand Prix of 1949 was won by a likeable young Lancastrian named Geoffrey Duke, who also finished second in the Junior race. Duke learned to ride a motorcycle during the war as a despatch rider, and afterwards rode in trials for some time before taking to road racing. His clean and stylish riding was immediately remarked, and led to his being adopted by the world's most famous racing teams, to his recognition as un-questionably the greatest rider of his day, to his almost universal adulation, to calumny and victimization, and to an OBE—in that chronological order. But all these are matters for the next chapter.

This chapter covers a wide span of years because the world war merely interrupted a chain of events that marked the emergence of a new school of motorcycle design. Throughout the period, motorcycles grew progressively safer, more controllable, more comfortable, better equipped and generally faster. Engine design was liberalized, frame design was revolutionized, while the social and economic pressures that engendered the cyclemotor and the scooter caused the motorcycle to become bastardized. Throughout the fourteen years, design was a fizzing ferment of fresh ideas and revised standards. The social background of motorcycling might be impossible adequately to describe, for every country suffered in its own peculiar way at one time or another if not throughout these years. But the new wave of motorcycle design was working up to its peak, ready to burgeon in the 1950s in a display of virtuosity that had never been seen before and that seems unlikely ever to be repeated again.

1950-1972
6 Back into the melting pot

There appears to be very little originality displayed in
modern motorcycle design, and I think it may be taken
as an axiom that where there is no originality there
is no progress.
George Lanchester

Plus ça change, plus c'est la même chose. The aphorism is so valid when applied to the motorcycle that it must be either an utter condemnation or a complete justification of the machine. In the years covered by this final chapter, the motorcycle, whether as a means of sport, of transport, of making a fortune, or of making progress, practically died, only to be reborn with such a display of vigour as to suggest that the experience must utterly have transformed it.

Amazingly, the motorcycle remains very much the same as it always has been. During this period a number of developments took place which started as extravaganzas and ended up among the commonplace: four-stroke engines sprouted three or four cylinders, high-performance two-strokes appeared with a like number, carburettors could be counted in numbers equalling those of the cylinders, disc brakes began to be worn and, for a while, streamlining too. Yet none of these things could be said to be new, every one having its counterpart in the near or distant history of motorcycling, as the preceding chapters will have shown; and none of them sufficed to alter the basic shape or even cast any doubt on the validity of the concept. The more the details changed, the more the basis stood out apparently immutable, and the more amazing did its survival appear.

Schiller once wrote that the world's history was the world's court of judgment. That being so, an historian must go very warily about usurping the world's perogative and pressing his own judgment on the events that have transpired, lest he merely judge them as he himself has seen them. When those events are themselves on the way to oblivion, any recollection is better than none; but when they are recent and fresh in the minds of many, there is no need for the jurors to stampede. A whole generation is spanned by this last chapter, while the history of motorcycling in that period has been so changeable and so inconclusive that such a lengthy period is hardly long enough to discover a course of development or evolution convincing enough to allow extrapolation into the future.

Feeling that one cannot see a satisfactory perspective if standing too close, the authors feel that a brief summary of the motorcycling world in the last two decades is the best way to conclude this work. We cannot examine it in too much detail, for it is as yet too soon to be sure which details are significant. The student may form his own opinions, and nothing but matters of fact need change them.

At the beginning of the 1950s a new wave of technical evolution became apparent in motorcycles. Many were the men who yearned for a mount that showed some signs of having been designed in the latter half of the twentieth century instead of bearing a crippling resemblance to the bicycles that owed their origins to the latter half of the nineteenth. As least as numerous, however, were those *laudatores temporis acti* who

The elements of a 1956 50 c.c. NSU sprinting (152)

could not or would not recognize science as a boon and progress as inevitable; so in many cases it was the modern designs that failed on the market, the staid oldfashioned ones that prevailed. In the words of Hazlitt, *There is not a more mean, stupid, dastardly, pitiful, selfish, spiteful, envious, ungrateful animal than the Public. It is the greatest of cowards, for it is afraid of itself.* Alas, too many of the motorcycling public were afraid of modernity: the war had put a temporary stop to it in 1939, the years of peaceful austerity had prevented its coming for a little longer; but when in 1950 the time was ripe for a fresh look at motorcycle design, the customers would have none of it.

This conservatism exhibited itself in different ways in different lands. The Germans held on to their generally rather slothful, rather curvaceous and admittedly well-made designs; the Italians were mostly committed to the idea that they all had the blood of that artistic old rogue Benvenuto Cellini in their veins, and contented themselves with exquisite metalwork and artistic, often astonishingly handsome, adaptations of designs that they had proved decades earlier; while the English pinned their faith on the big banger and did their best to bask in the glory earned by that finest of vintage motorcycles, the Manx Norton.

These national attitudes were not adopted without modification by the racing fraternity, except in England. The result was that the Norton, while performing far better than it had any right to expect, found itself faced with increasingly formidable competition from abroad. What gave the Norton its new lease of life, and enabled it to hold its own

164

Reg Armstrong, 1951 Senior—AJS Porcupine 500 V-twin **(153)**

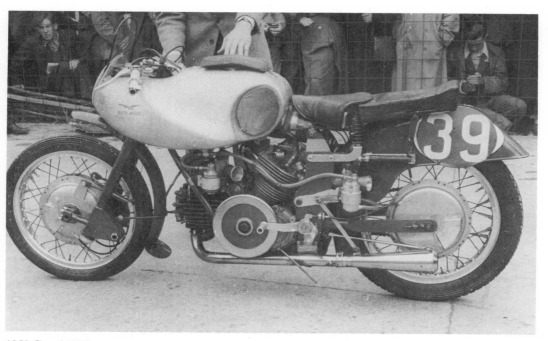

1950 Guzzi **(154)**

so remarkably, was its new frame, nicknamed the Featherbed. It was simple, it was beautiful, and it was (especially in the critical area around the steering head) extremely effective in retaining the bicycle parts in that precise relationship which alone ensures good navigational properties. Appearing in 1950, the Featherbed gave a very good account of itself, particularly in the hands of the youthful Geoffrey Duke, whose compliment to it must surely remain one of the best on record: offered a seat by a BBC interviewer after his 1950 TT win, Duke simply said: 'No thanks, I've been lying down all the morning!'

It did not take long, though, for the opposition to adopt the style of the Norton frame, and then the Birmingham firm was really up against it. The Gilera four was going from strength to strength, and the similar four from MV Agusta was rapidly getting through its teething troubles. Both these Italian machines were replete with well-mannered power, and anyone accustomed to the chronic megaphonitis of a big racing single would have marvelled in their docility. Indeed, the Gilera mechanics might well borrow one of the fours to pop down to the village for some shopping, the 'fire engine' proving perfectly tractable at a fraction of its normal revs and throttle openings; while the infant son of Les Graham would be perched by his father astride the tank of the big MV, and take the machine pottering round the paddock while papa acted as ballast and neutral-finder.

By contrast, Moto Guzzi took the course of least resistance, as it were, by designing bicycles that needed less engine power for a given degree of performance. That they succeeded may be measured not only in their string of racing successes but also in their prodigiously good fuel economy, Fergus Anderson recording that they commonly got better than 35 m.p.g. from the racing 350. Guzzi had a full-size wind-tunnel that was used to good purpose, and Guzzi streamlining was always of the best. The machines were also very light (the weight of a finishing coat of gloss paint was not allowed on the fairings) and had a very small frontal area. In fact the 1954 Guzzi Bialbero (twin camshaft) racer was, with its special cage frame integrated with the full frontal fairing, its transverse cylindrical fuel tank strapped low beneath a pair of shaped wooden blocks, and its double coil ignition for the oversquare engine whose downdraught carburettor had a typically Guzzi bore like a sousaphone, probably the most scientifically devised racer of the era, and perhaps of all time.

Running it a good second in this respect in the early 'fifties was the NSU, which was not only tolerably well faired, beautifully made and superbly detailed in its cycle parts, but also boasted an engine that in terms of volumetric efficiency was without peer. In sober fact, the Rennsport NSU was the first and for a long time the only unblown petrol motor developing 125 b.h.p. per litre. Probably the only thing to rival it in this way was the blown nitro-burning 500 that NSU kept for domestic race meetings, where the Germans still revelled in supercharging—of BMWs as well, one need hardly add. But in the international events it was the unblown 250 twin and its half-size brother that brought NSU the Lightweight and Ultra-Lightweight Championships on more than one occasion, their team of gifted riders being led by Werner Haas, who was killed in a flying accident in 1956.

Guzzi and NSU between them epitomized the two important developments that in 1954 heightened an already marked upward trend in race speeds since the introduction of the Norton frame. These things were the general adoption of streamlining and the great step forward in the extraction of power from an engine of a given displacement. 1954 was the year when the lap record for the Lightweight TT was increased by a margin greater than ever before.

166

Ray Amm winning the 1953 Senior on his Norton (155)

R. L. Graham (MV Agusta), second in the 1952 Senior (156)

Progress was rapid in those fitful, fateful years. Streamlining grew from a tiny fairing that enveloped the steering head and swept back beneath the rider's forearms, first into a dolphin-beaked enclosure of the engine and fuel tank, and then into the full 'dustbin' —a bullet-shaped enclosure that hid everything forward of the rider's shins, with a curvaceous windscreen above. Brakes suddenly found they had more work to do, because the streamlined bicycles were going much faster (the 'fire engines' were good for well over 150 m.p.h. on some circuits) and suffered from less 'induced headwind' to act as a brake when the throttle was closed. So brakes became larger, often being duplicated on the front wheel, and were more positively ventilated since the dustbin fairing tended to deprive them of the wind in the willows that hitherto had sufficed to keep them cool.

Probably the most wonderful year ever for motorcycle racing was 1957, when all the great makes were locked in combat, with the exception of NSU. It was the last year in which full streamlining was permitted, it was the year when the Senior TT was stretched to eight laps, when the Island was first lapped at over 100 m.p.h. (by Bob McIntyre on a Gilera), when Europe echoed to the sounds of singles, twins, fours and even an eight— the fabulous V8 Guzzi 500. The Gileras were practically invincible, but the private owners did very well on their Nortons—which was no doubt better for business (if not for the future) as far as Norton themselves were concerned, the firm having by then withdrawn from racing a works team.

Perhaps it was all too good to last. Perhaps a brief flurry of contention is all that is needed from time to time. Perhaps, again, times were proving too hard for the expense of racing to be commercially justifiable. Anyway, racing went into a decline after 1957, with all the great Italian firms withdrawing their support.

Then after a couple of years there appeared from the east a cloud no bigger than a man's hand. A young Japanese company called Honda had built some enterprising and in some respects original 125 racers, and entered them in the TT just to see how they would get on. They did not win; but they all finished, every one of them, in line ahead on the results table from fifth place downwards. Somehow, few people in Europe seemed to take them seriously.

Within two more years everybody was taking Honda very seriously indeed. The company had waxed almightily, and was doing tremendous export business all over the world, and their four-cylinder racing 250 was pulverizing the opposition at every international race meeting. Some of the opposition was not too faint-hearted, notably that from Italy, but broadly speaking, Honda were supreme. European ears that had mourned the absence of that rich and kaleidophonic howl from the Gilera and MV fours now thrilled to the shriek of the Hondas as they trumpeted up to their 14,000 r.p.m. peak. There was something new for Europeans to mourn: the fact that there was nothing to rival these shrill Japanese multis. A few quite effective twins and singles were still being made, but the situation was summed up by McIntyre in 1961 when he was riding for Honda in the Lightweight class, for Bianchi in the Junior, and for Glaswegian tuner-entrant Joe Potts on a rather special Norton in the Senior. Asked about the problems of changing from one to another, he replied that the most noticeable difference was in speed: 'You go from the 250 to the slower Bianchi and then to an even slower Norton.' As it happened, that was the year when the Lightweight TT lap record was bumped up again by as great a margin as in 1954.

The days of the big single seemed numbered in top-flight racing. Everywhere the trend was to smaller cylinders and more of them, to ever higher rates of revolution (Ducati produced a very successful desmodromic valve gear that was worth an extra 4,000 r.p.m.),

168

Veteran World Champion congratulates new star. In 1955 young John Surtees (*left*) was beginning to assert himself against Geoff Duke **(157)**

W. Lomas (Guzzi) at Quarter Bridge in the 1955 Junior **(158)**

to a multiplicity of gears in the transmission. Honda were the archetypes, but there were many others. Those designers who jibbed at the thought of myriad hordes of tiny valves tried the alternative two-stroke concept and, with the aid of such devices as the disc valve, made it work. Bultaco in Spain, DKW in West Germany, MZ in East Germany, and Yamaha in Japan all worked up their two-strokes to racing levels of performance (if not of reliability) and entered the lists with notable success. There even appeared a class for racers of only 50 c.c., and before long they were established and going places fast— usually at astronomical and virtually constant revs, the riders playing virtuoso tunes on gear-levers that might, as in the Kreidler, offer as many as twelve ratios.

The fact that, relatively speaking, the 50s did so well compared with the 500s suggests that something was wrong somewhere. Such was indeed the case: the governing bodies of racing steadfastly refused to allow any developments involving fuel, stream-lining, or even basic concept. Within this strait-jacket, racing became a mere horse-power race. Engines went screaming up to ever higher revs, developing their power in ever narrowing portions of the rev range, needing more and more gears in consequence, more and more fuel, more and more skill. All the successful 'bikes had the same sort of frames, the same sort of fairings, the same sort of transmission. Everybody's concern was with b.h.p., and when every rider could summon about the same power as every other then the whole affair degraded into a pointless scratching match. Before long, radio commentaries on major international motorcycle races began to ignore the makes of the machines taking part and to concentrate wholly on the names and fortunes of the riders—a sure sign that nothing of any importance was happening.

The ordered fatuity of modern racing (and this applied as much to scrambling and to trials) had nothing to offer the world but danger. Admittedly there were some improve-ments in tyres in the mid-1960s, and these contributed to an increase in speed and to better utilization of power. Otherwise there were no bright spots in the evolution of the high-performance motorcycle, and had not been for years and years: the whole futile business was an ever changing picture of men in search of power instead of learning how best to utilize power.

An important tyre development was the change in profile. Bob McIntyre, who did much of the tyre testing for Dunlops, had a curious riding style, one feature of which was a sudden peremptory laying-down of the 'bike for a corner and an equally smart reversion to upright on the way out, rather than a smooth progression from upright to full bank and back. This encouraged Dunlops to develop tyres of approximately tri-angular cross-section. They had found that the traditional circular-section tyre wore unevenly in racing; in trying to make a tyre which started out as those tyres had finished, they produced angled flat sections on each side of the tread centre point that gave additional tread area and additional grip when the bike was banked over to extreme angles of lean.

The other important tyre development of the period was also British, originating from another manufacturer, Avon. They concentrated more on the development of tread compounds which gave much more grip, especially on wet roads, than the natural rubber that had been normal wear in the preceding seventy years or so. Finding ways of exploiting modern synthetic rubbers (notably styrene butadyene) they led a revolution in polymer chemistry that has not yet subsided, having spread to car tyres throughout the world and promising to extend to other vehicles as well.

On this evidence, motorcycle racing could at least claim to have done some good in the world. Not even such little progress as this could be claimed by other forms of motor-

The American scene. Harley-Davidson, as active and successful as ever—on the track, and (*over*) hill-climbing (**159–160**)

cycle sport, yet they blossomed as classic road racing withered. For the sensation-seeking spectator, and indeed for the rider who was fit enough and brave enough, there seemed to be more excitement and diversity in scrambling, the cross-country rough-riding sport that now enjoyed a startling rise in popularity and seduced many a motorcyclist from his devotion to the thoroughbred road machine. And for those whose temperament, physique, or fortune, denied either kind of sport there were still the traditional trials which every weekend tempted handfuls of sensitive-handed riders out into some of the most beautiful hill country available, where they set themselves to overcome rocks and rivers, loam and leaf mould, and all the obstacles that nature and the organizers' whims might combine to produce.

Alas, racing had lost not only much of its point but also many of its finest men. Anderson, Graham, Haas, McIntyre, all these had gone; so had the slightly built, very brave Rhodesian Ray Amm, killed on his Norton in 1955 at Imola; and Dickie Dale, the man whom everybody sought whenever there was a new big man-eater to be tamed, —MV, Gilera, Guzzi, BMW, he rode them all—met his end on the Nürburgring in 1961. But at least we may rejoice that the two most outstanding riders of the 'fifties, Duke and Surtees, are still with us.

Geoffrey Duke, born in 1923 at St Helens in Lancashire, has already been mentioned briefly. Anything less than a biography would be too brief to do him justice. Let us say that he was indisputably the greatest rider of his day; a man who on a motorcycle had an impeccable style and off it had manners and modesty to match; a man who had the sort of temperament that allowed him mildly to turn the other cheek to catastrophe, but to fight like a tiger while any breath of hope remained. In 1953, when it became hopeless for him to keep up with the fast Italians by risking his neck more on every corner, he joined the Gilera team (taking Avon tyres with him) and reached the pinnacle of his success with them in 1955, by which time he had been a member of the OBE for four years. He retired from racing in 1959.

A similar transition from Norton to an Italian four, this time the MV Agusta, characterized the motorcycling career of John Surtees, a far less tidy but no less tigerish rider. Starting racing with immediate success in 1951, he joined the Norton team in 1955, signed for Count Agusta the following year, and notched up a formidable succession of victories before retiring from motorcycle racing to become one of the most outstanding car drivers of the present day, the only man to be a World Champion on two wheels and on four.

Others who made the same switch from two wheels to four were not always as fortunate. Gary Hocking, who had partnered Surtees in the MV Agusta team, and stayed on for a couple of years to partner Mike Hailwood, decided to give up motorcycle racing and take to cars because they were less dangerous. Ironically he killed himself in a racing car in 1962. Bob Armstrong made the change more successfully and was well known as the last of the real privateers in Grand Prix car racing in the early years of the three-litre formula (which began its run in 1966) but eventually killed himself while practising in his Brabham. These two were in many ways typical of that band of hard-riding colonials who included Amm, Phillis (also killed in 1962), Coleman, Kavanagh and Redman, all of whom enlivened post-war racing considerably—Redman in particular showing great talent for effective race tactics and shrewd judgment of pace with the result that he won six world championships in four years, a number of world records, and the MBE, before going into a second retirement after his first in 1959.

Nor were the Italians wanting in talent in the early 1950s: it was only after the retirement of such as Ubbiali (with nine world championships), Milani, Masetti, Lorenzetti and Dulio Agostini that they seemed to go into eclipse for a while, though in the 'sixties Provini, Pasolini and Giacomo Agostini displayed a rare mixture of genius and courage to bring them out of it again.

For all the efforts of these men, the ten years from 1955 to 1965 were years of attrition in racing, with more and more firms backing out of the arena. They were likewise years of attrition in the industry, with more and more firms disappearing from the competition not only of the arena but also of the market place, and only the young Japanese companies prospering. It would have been difficult to forecast this in 1950, when all the great factories of the world were getting into production with machines that at last were beginning to look modern. Vertical twins were blossoming all around, lightweights were improving enormously, frames were being sprung, strokes shortened, forks telescoped and ignitions coiled in every factory in the business—except, of course, those of Vincent, Indian and Harley Davidson, who all had their reasons for continuing in their severally egregious ways.

But this brief flurry of progress did not endure. Motorcycles were getting a bad name, and their unpopularity led to an ostracism that proved a punishment not well suited to the crime. In America, Britain and Europe, the gentleman rider was not much in evidence, and the day of the 'cowboy' was upon us, his choice perhaps a Gold Star BSA or a Bonneville Triumph, with which a young fellow might introduce either a little life or else the fear of God into his smug suburban surroundings.

Some suburbanites represent the majority of every land, however, and they were duly outraged. Nor did they bother to distinguish between motorcyclists and that equally unruly but somewhat more effete mob who plagued the roads with swarming scooters. Anything on two wheels was vilified. In this atmosphere, the British motorcycle industry could not flourish. Scooters and lightweights might still abound, but the 'real' motorcycles were disappearing fast. Vincent, Sunbeam, Douglas, the big Ariels, all went to the wall, and did not go alone. Gradually the big singles disappeared, leaving only Velocette. The only man-size 'bikes to remain were the Clubmen-type roadsters, the high-performance super-sporting (sometimes pseudo-racing) mounts like the BSA Rocket Gold Star, the Triumph T120 Bonneville, the Velocette Venom (particularly nice), the Norton SS, and the heavier, quieter, slower BMW best represented by the 600 c.c. R69S. In the 'fifties, there had been some other splendid and successful sporting models such as the Gold Star BSA single, the NSU Sportmax, the Series D Vincents with the first production fairings, and—best conceived of the lot as far as the paper specification went—the 90 Plus Douglas. But they had all gone.

Taking their place was a rash of new lightweight machinery, encouraged by discriminating legislation. Some of these were little imitations of the real thing, such as the hotter 175 and 250 c.c. Ducatis, the Royal Enfield Crusader Sports and its progeny, or the very fast and controllable Aermacchi—an Italian near-racer that owed its continued existence to Harley-Davidson. On the other hand, there were some new ideas taking shape about what should be expected of a motorcycle, and the fully-enclosed, sprightly and marvellously handleable Ariel Leader seemed to usher in a revolution. So it should have—but Ariel did better business when they produced a 'naked' sports version called the Arrow, which was mechanically almost identical to the 250 c.c. two-stroke Leader twin but was far less sophisticated and about £30 cheaper. Perhaps motorcyclists did not want car-type comforts. Cars were easily obtained by those who did; too easily, for there were now too many cars on the road for the comfort of the more vulnerable motor-

Wilhelm Noll before his 1955 World Record attack. His 500 c.c. BMW developed 75 b.h.p. at 8,000 r.pm. **(161)**

Formidable pair in 1964—Deubel and Horner, BMW **(162)**

cyclist. Still, there were some car-owner's amenities that the monotrack-addict fancied: electric starters were by 1960 a feasible proposition for the smaller fashionable engines, and were being fitted as standard to the smart, well-finished Hondas, Yamahas and Suzukis that began to swamp the markets of the world.

The greatest of these by then and ever since was Honda, with an output of more than a million machines in 1962. Admittedly the majority of these were mere mopeds, admittedly 84 per cent of the total production stayed at home—but remembering that the company only began functioning fourteen years earlier, it is difficult to see this rags-to-riches story as anything but a vindication of Honda's concept of selling more than just basic transport to the commuter and more than mere brute power to the enthusiast. As he himself expressed it: 'It is important to create products which will arouse a big demand, rather than study the demand before going into production.' In other words it is a matter of *creating* markets, not just satisfying markets.

A little more than a year after the end of the war, Soichiro Honda set himself up in a wooden hut on a bomb site in Hamamatsu to produce one moped a day. He had been a motor mechanic and a successful racing driver and motorcyclist—until he crashed and decided that perhaps it was not such a promising career after all. The moped that he built with twelve assistants and some ropey old machine tools was a poor thing and not entirely his own, for its engine was an army surplus job which was converted to run on fuel extracted from the roots of pine trees. In chaotic post-war Japan, where there were very few vehicles and very little petrol, it was better than nothing; and lively sales bore no relation whatever to its merit. Soon the supply of army communications engines dried up, and Honda built a 50 c.c. two-stroke to be attached to an ordinary pedal cycle. Once again success was immediate. It was enough to justify the establishment of the Honda Motor Company, or strictly, the Honda Technical and Research Manufacturing Company, with a capital of $2,777. This took place in September 1948, and within a year more designs had been put on the market, including two that qualified for description as motorcycles. Honda himself had designed them, but he found an exceptionally competent salesman named Fujisawa to develop the company's marketing policy, and in another four years Honda was Japan's biggest motorcycle producer. The firm now showed enough promise to justify the faith of the Japanese Government in lending the money to buy a million dollars' worth of modern machine tools.

Seldom can such a loan have been repaid so quickly. By 1957 Honda was an exporter (of five machines!) and ten years later exported about 600,000. That was the year when the USA imported half a million motorcycles; and a lot of them were Hondas.

The way Honda wooed a new market in America was an object lesson to all. Advertisements in the specialized motorcycling journals could be taken for granted, but Honda advertised elsewhere in car magazines, sports magazines, glamour journals, women's journals, girls' journals, university and college periodicals, commercial radio programmes for youngsters. Honda had found that 30 per cent of their machines were bought by people under 19 years of age, and they went after such people assiduously, without forgetting the more censorious older generation who were placated by the famous slogan 'You meet the nicest people on a Honda'.

It was all very suave and sophisticated; but then so were the motorcycles. English and European manufacturers were bleating away with excuses about it being a poor market, that these were hard times, that the riding public was not sophisticated enough to demand or expect the technical novelties that lay about waiting to be exploited. But this was sheer muddled thinking, cart before the horse, the market for such people having

176

The rougher side of scrambling. Greeves, BSA, and Cotton splash through (163)

vanished because they were tired of the lack of sophisticated machinery and had taken their custom elsewhere. Meanwhile, it was mainly the Japanese, to whom overhead camshafts and electric starters savoured not of madness nor yet of degeneracy, whose motorcycles were flooding the USA where two-wheeling was booming.

The Americans took to motorcycling with all the obsessive enthusiasm and fast-learnt competence that they had displayed in the past decade over imported sportscars. The dirty leather-jacketed layabouts were still to be encountered here and there; but despite them the two-wheeler became socially acceptable and caught on fast. Even New York City allotted plenty of parking spots for motorcycles, which abounded in the suburbs. The emphasis there seemed to be largely on small-capacity Japs, although there was a good sprinkling of hairy-chested fellows astride things like the Atlas (a Norton Dominator enlarged to a thumping 750 c.c.) or the BSA Rocket Gold Star which was a 650 twin in something like a Gold Star frame. Likewise there was a coterie of enthusiasts for the big BMW. However, the general tendency of the American motorcyclist in the early 1960s was to go in for tiddlers, probably due entirely to the fact that the Japanese (who were the principle source of machinery) had not so far made anything else.

Yet America is a big place and there can hardly be a country better suited to a fine big solo. Even though many of the roads in the USA are policed in a way that makes the Kremlin sound like Liberty Hall, there are compensations, especially in those regions where the climate is highly predictable and the scenery as like as not breathtaking. In such territory, what better way of covering the ground than on a motorcycle?

Of course, if the idea of travelling is just to go gallumping along some turnpike, looking neither to right nor to left but slogging on into the wild blue yonder, there might be something to be said (for Americans) for being frantically all-American on a third of a ton of Harley-Davidson. It was becoming evident, however, that the utter banality of these mighty Würlitzers was becoming as obvious to the native element as was their sheer impracticality for most of the aims of motorcycling. Old habits die hard, alas: before long the Americans were to embark on a quest for sheer power such as was to alter, and arguably to corrupt, motorcycle design with a thoroughness that transcended the magnificent and verged on the alarming.

Whatever ambitions might be fulfilled in the land of private enterprise, no such lust for power could have any hope of satisfaction in the countries of the Communist bloc. Russia was producing nondescript motorcycles for strictly utilitarian purposes, but it was in the countries of Eastern Europe that some semblance of sparkle and variety in design persisted. The variety might have been greater had not the directors of the nationalized vehicle industry of Eastern Germany decided that all its efforts should be concentrated on the development of two-stroke engines for cars and motorcycles alike. The effect of this was to put an end to the quite long run of the four-stoke 250 c.c. Simson, built at a factory near Erfurt first as a tourer and later as a quite sprightly and handsome sporting machine. The last one was made in 1962, and thereafter it was a rationalized two-stroke or nothing. The Sperber (Sparrowhawk) was a 75 c.c. lightweight with a four-speed gearbox and 50 m.p.h. potential, and the rationalization idea dictated the availability of an alternative engine of 50 c.c. The same principle was applied to the products of the MZ factory which used to be the home of the illustrious DKW at Zschopau. Quantity production of two models was diversified by the availability of two different engine sizes for each: thus the 125 and 150 c.c. MZ machines were virtually identical except for their cylinder bore dimensions. The same differentiation produced a 175 and a 250. Limited production of sidecar and trials machines made up the MZ

Towards a world record—Bob Leppan (164)

range in the factory where the brilliant two-stroke engineer Walter Kaaden had perfected the disc valve which made the racing MZ two-stroke almost irresistible in the lightweight and ultra-lightweight classes a few years earlier—though for all their speed they never won a world championship.

Other Eastern European countries had their own machines whose speed and stamina might not always suffice to put them on the racing map but invariably went a long way towards earning victory in such events as the International Six Days' Trial. In Czechoslovakia there were CZ and Jawa, both of them in great demand for sporting use, CZ being particularly successful in international trials. Hungary produced the OSA, the SHL and the Junak. All of them were two-strokes and only the Jawa was available with an engine of more than 250 c.c., although in the 1950s MZ had made a 350 twin.

For a time it seemed as though small utilitarian machines such as these would dominate motorcycling. Within the Communist area, small machines were justified on ideological grounds. Elsewhere, ultra-lightweights and mopeds—every one looking like a Honda except the Suzuki which looked like a Yamaha—were the invariable choice of those who rode as much because they had to as because they wanted to. The big banger, it seemed, had only one utilitarian application, as a police mount: Harleys in America, a variety of Triumphs, Nortons and BSAs in Britain and a lot of other countries, BMWs in Germany, and in France those handsome Ratier flat twins that were for a while exclusive to the French police before disappearing entirely, whereupon BMW took their place.

179

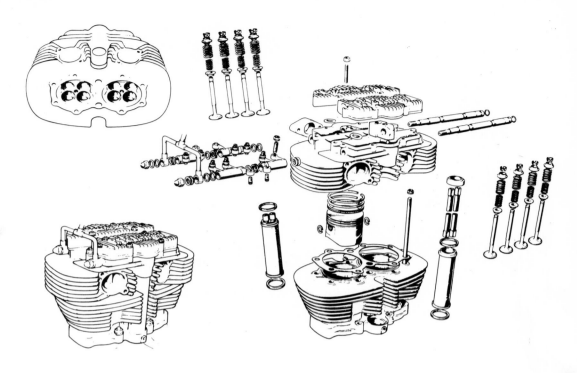

In the 1960s the British tried madly to keep their big parallel twins competitive. Weslake devised this 8-valve conversion for the 650 Triumph (165)

A few sporting riders who were sufficiently positive or sufficiently indifferent to persist with big machines still had their very snappy twins and a small but steadily growing market could be discerned for specialized hybrids such as that peculiarly English machine the Triton. This consisted of a Triumph twin engine in a Norton featherbed frame, and was at its best when built by such specialists as Geoff Monty and Dudley Ward, or the even smaller Dresda firm of Dave Degens—all of them British racing men. Lower down in the capacity scale were the boys' sportsters, peppery lightweights of which some had more performance than many a man could handle: Bultaco from Spain, Ducati from Italy, Yamaha and Honda from Japan.

One might have expected the Ariel Arrow to have a place in such company, but it had gone. The British industry was moribund. Every kind of rationalization was tried. Associated Motor Cycles, which used to comprise AJS and Matchless in London, found themselves combined with Norton from Birmingham, Francis Barnett from Coventry, and James from Greet. Before long only Norton remained, soon to combine with Villiers (who had been a competitor for AMC) and set up afresh with many protestations about lively marketing and advanced engineering and nothing to show but latter-day versions of the Dominator Twin. Alas, the big 750 c.c. Atlas had been too much of a

A. Butscher and passenger W. Kalauch (492 BMW) accelerate from Governor's Bridge on to the finish straight in the 1964 Side-car TT **(166)**

thumper for its own good, and something pretty drastic was necessary to stop it breaking itself: the answer came in the new Norton Commando, basically similar but with an ingenious frame design (named Isolastic) in which rubber bushes provided a measure of compliance which effectively isolated the vibratory elements from the rider without doing anything to cure the vibration at source. The rider no longer had to dismount every 150 miles to rest from the tingling that numbed his senses and played havoc with his circulation. Instead, he merely had to dismount every 200 miles or so in order to replace the exhaust pipes in the cylinder head ports whence vibration had shaken them loose. This was progress!

The BSA-Triumph amalgam, riding on the back of the market as usual, was content in the mid-'sixties to give its various models an annual face lift and to appeal to the brand loyalties of established customers by producing the same machines with different badges according to the dealerships to which they were to be entrusted. Looking for new customers was apparently not part of their business—and indeed the UK market, which stood at around 80,000 machines for the year 1965, has not grown noticeably since. As for the few remaining independent firms, Royal Enfield and Velocette simply dug their heads into the sand and carried on vainly scratching, though the latter firm did at least have some precision engineering work as the mainstay of its business while motorcycle sales dwindled. It was the same story again: only the established Velocette enthusiast was likely to buy a new Velocette—and this was perhaps a pity, for the 500 c.c. Velocette Venom, especially in its Clubman's-racer Thruxton form, was a beautifully made and nicely finished classical pushrod single which had an unmistakable style about it to complement performance that (for a 500 single) was pretty good. Moreover its stamina was unimpeachable; but this was not enough to keep it competitive, and by the end of 1971 Velocette had finished, as had Royal Enfield whose big vertical-twin Constellation had been kept in limited production in an underground factory for far more years than its design or performance really merited.

The traditionalist and the historian may mourn the demise of so many great machines and great names. Yet half-way through the 1960s there was no real evidence of sterility and in numerical terms there had never before been a period like it. The tremendous motorcycling boom in the USA promised to find an echo in Europe, and there looked to be a bright future for top-notch big machines as well as sprightly little town traffic-cheaters. In closing the first edition of this book we quoted Hazlitt again: *If this world were good for nothing else, it is a fine subject for speculation.* That was late in 1965; a year or two more and we could have observed the burgeoning of a whole new class of luxury high-performance motorcycles, as a dozen or so manufacturers all around the world turned their speculations into metal.

The first of these actually appeared in 1965 and was met with some consternation and not a little dismay. This was the Honda CB450, apparently a big vertical twin cast in the traditional British mould and therefore apparently a technological throwback after the exquisitely refined lightweights that Honda had made a speciality. The fact that it was advertised as a rival to the Triumph Bonneville did nothing to encourage us; but an inspection of its design and specification showed that the resemblances were entirely superficial. It may have been big and ugly and heavy like a British big twin— indeed it was actually heavier than the 650 Bonneville, despite having an engine of only 444 c.c.— but the detail design of the engine was little short of revolutionary. Despite a fairly short stroke it was a tall engine and carried a very long timing chain to drive its two overhead camshafts. The cam lobes on these were very large and were drilled to give a pressure oil feed directly to the lobe faces, though it took some time for this feed to become fully effective when starting from cold. The cam followers took the form of lever tappets mounted on a shaft parallel to the camshaft, and below this shaft was a parallel torsion bar from which an arm extended to the tip of the valve stem. The combination of cam profiles and torsion bar springs allowed the engine to function without any mis-behaviour of the valve gear at up to 12,000 r.p.m., giving it an enormous margin of safety beyond the 8,500 at which it developed no less than 43 b.h.p. Such specific power, nearly 100 b.h.p. per litre, had in earlier days been associated only with the most thoroughgoing racing machinery, yet here was a flexible, quiet, mild-mannered touring machine combining plenty of punch with easy manners and even an electric starter. It was by no means perfect, for the dampers and suspension geometry debased the handling somewhat and the ratios of the four-speed gearbox were not well matched to the engine. Still, the CB450 (christened The Black Bomber) pointed the way motorcycles were likely to go in the future, and it was obvious from looking at previous Honda examples that the few shortcomings in its make-up could and would be rectified before long.

An even bigger motorcycle emerged from Italy late in 1965. This was the 700 c.c. Guzzi V7, a heavyweight luxury tourer whose V-twin engine was transversely mounted in a rather ramshackle frame, and communicated to the rear wheel by shaft drive. The engine was derived from one that had been developed by Guzzi to suit a military specification for a go-anywhere lightweight three-wheeled vehicle, and it was therefore reasonable to expect unusual durability and ease of maintenance. This expectation was to be justified in due course as the machine grew to 750 c.c. and eventually to 850, with a super-sports 750 in a better frame doing well in competition, but not before Guzzi had hedged their bet on the sporting market by getting good contracts for supplying these motorcycles to the police and the army.

In the following year another big Italian twin came on the scene. This was the Laverda, built in a factory that was a converted country mansion. The proprietor was the son of a wealthy industrialist, and his unashamed design inspiration was the little Honda CB77. The Laverda looked remarkably similar though much bigger. It also cost a great deal more, but it was made with such care and attention to detail that no careful

Paul Dunstall's twin-disc brake
on Triumph 750 Trident (167)

critic could fail to be impressed. Starting as a 600 c.c. twin, it soon grew to 750, and its proprietory Grimeca brakes were replaced by big double drums of Laverda's own design which seemed to fill the 18-inch wheels and were evidently necessary to haul back the considerable weight of the machine from the very high speeds it could reach. The Laverda was powerful from the beginning, but as the years went by it was developed into a high-performance bicycle of real competitiveness, and as a tourer it covered the ground most compulsively. The manufacturers insisted that it was not a short-distance scratcher but were happy to see it used for long-distance racing in the events which began to proliferate for production machines, and in the more strenuous of these such as the twenty-four hours events at Barcelona and Paris the Laverda did very well indeed. It felt much lighter and handled much better than its true weight might lead one to expect, giving the rider every encouragement to deploy the full power (over 60 b.h.p. in the later versions) and ride it at full speed (119 m.p.h., or more for the competition version) for miles on end. It is a lusty bike, a tireless bike and one replete with beautiful details; but there is one item missing, for the Laverda shares with the Guzzi the distinction of having no kick-starter pedal, relying implicitly on a powerful electric motor and large battery.

Also making a tentative appearance on the Italian scene in 1966 was a roadgoing version of the celebrated MV Agusta 4. Enlarged to 600 c.c., softened by having only two carburettors and a well-silenced twin-tailpipe exhaust system, it was presented as an essentially touring motorcycle, not a super-sports job as might have been expected. Nevertheless it was decently quick, every bit as smooth as could be expected, and it was taken a further step out of the ordinary by being given twin mechanically-operated disc brakes on its front wheels.

Indeed 1966 may be called the year of the disc brake. Several versions appeared in Britain, either twin hydraulically-operated discs based on designs of Colin Lyster or a big single-disc design developed by Lockheed and fitted to a number of racing machines. The Lockheed disc also found a place on the front wheel of the 'Street' Métisse, this beautiful roadster being the first road-going motorcycle to feature an hydraulically operated disc brake. Métisse is a French word signifying a mongrel bitch; but this very English motorcycle was the latest product of the Rickman brothers who had made themselves a considerable name in scrambling with machines of somewhat mixed ancestry, in which Triumph engines and BSA frames played no little part. By this stage, however, they were making their own elegant chassis in which a choice of engines might be installed, and the resemblance between roadsters and racers was at once deliberate and encouraging. It was another small specialist, Paul Dunstall, who was attracted by the Lyster double-disc brake. This he employed in some of his customized motorcycles, which at that time were based on current Norton and Triumph designs. Dunstall had once been a notable short-circuit racer, enjoying considerable success with the Norton Domiracer which was a last-ditch effort by Norton to remain competitive in racing by supertuning their Dominator o.h.v. twin after the classical Manx single had gone out of production. Norton did not persevere with their efforts, and Dunstall took over all the Domiracer stocks; but he soon found that the most rewarding market was the American one for customized high-performance roadsters, and he set himself to meet his demands with such thoroughness that before long the British Board of Trade categorized him as a manufacturer in his own right, so much of his machines being specially made rather than bought out. One of the most interesting features was the balance pipe in the exhaust system: this had been devised originally by the Triumph development engineer Doug Hele and was to be copied somewhat blindly by a number of others in the future. Dunstall however did the job properly, as Hele had done; the balance pipe between the two exhaust pipes was fitted as close as possible to the exhaust ports, and downstream from this junction the exhaust pipe's diameter was reduced. The effect was to enable the peak power associated with short exhaust pipes to be combined with the low speed torque produced by long pipes, and this flexibility stood Dunstall Nortons in very good stead when they were used competitively. His own efforts were confined to producing machines to attack the one-hour record, success being achieved at something like 130 m.p.h.

In real top-flight racing, Honda were supreme as ever. By 1966 they were encountering doughty opposition from the two-strokes in the 125 class, but on the other hand they were making themselves competitive in the 500 class—and indeed they are to this day the only company to have won every solo class of the TT. They did not, of course, compete in the sidecar class where, in the 1960s, it was usually taken for granted that this was a BMW monopoly.

Spanish Grand Prix 1964. Jim Redman (250 Honda Four) pursued by Tarquinio Provini (Benelli Four) **(168)**

Next pages: Hugh Anderson, 125 c.c. Suzuki, Spain 1964 **(169)**; and German Grand Prix, Nurbürgring, 1965. Derek Woodman, 125 c.c. MZ **(170)**

It was frequently assumed that the 500 class was an MV Agusta monopoly too, and the waning fortunes of the famous four-cylinder 'fire engines' had prompted Count Agusta to reassert himself with a new three-cylinder machine that was considerably lighter and lower and which exploited four valves per cylinder (after the example of Honda) to realize very high power outputs with fair reliability.

How they all compared and how thay all fared in the classical events of the 1966 season is most conveniently illustrated by the records of the Isle of Man TT Races. The 250 race was utterly dominated by Hailwood riding a 6-cylinder 24-valve 7-speed Honda. His standing-start lap of the Island established a class record at 104·29 m.p.h., after which he eased off to win at a leisurely 101·79. Second, on another Honda at 97·49 m.p.h. was Stewart Graham, that very same son of the late Les Graham whose introduction to the control of high-speed motorcycles was recorded early in this chapter. Third, at 91·49 m.p.h., was a Villiers special two-stroke ridden by their development engineer Peter Inchley. The discrepancies in speeds say all that is necessary.

It was to be expected that the 350 race would have been faster, for a needle match between the Honda of Hailwood and the MV of Agostini was eagerly anticipated; but the Honda failed early and the MV toured in to win at 100·87 after lapping at 103·09—and the second place went to an AJS at 93·83. . . . In the senior race the Honda-MV duel was a little more convincing but at this stage the MV was not yet a full 500, giving away 80 c.c. to the Honda and not quite able to make up for it despite Agostini's characteristically brilliant riding. Rain slowed the event down in the later stages, but Hailwood won on his four-cylinder Honda at 103·11 after establishing a record lap of over 107 m.p.h., while Agostini finished second at 101·9.

In the 125 class, Honda's fortunes were at a low ebb. They had replaced their four-cylinder 18,000 r.p.m. machines of the previous year by five-cylinder designs which revved at well over 20,000, but they were no match for the two-stroke twins of Yamaha and Suzuki. The late and brilliant Bill Ivy led Phil Read home in a Yamaha one-two followed by Suzuki's team leader, Hugh Anderson, and the best that Honda could do was to finish sixth. The news that Yamaha were developing a water-cooled four-cylinder two-stroke gave a sign of what was to come. In the little 50 c.c. class at least Honda could still keep their four-strokes ahead of the Suzuki two-strokes. Indeed there were no other makes represented, the field consisting of eleven Hondas (two works twins and nine singles) and six Suzukis, some of which were twin-cylinder twelve-speeders and the remainder the previous year's singles. The results sheet read Honda-Honda-Suzuki-Suzuki with the winner averaging 85·66 m.p.h.

When are we going to have a world beater again? wailed the British motorcycling journals. None of them seemed to have any idea who would do it or how it should be done, but amidst all the protest emerged the news that there was a project being hatched by the Manx Tourist Board to run a lottery, the proceeds of which would help BRM and Velocette to combine their talents to produce the necessary machine. The idea was, of course, that BRM should produce the engine, based on their experience with Grand Prix racing cars, and that Velocette should make the bicycle; but there were many who forecast that the probable outcome of such a liaison could only be a little less catastrophic than if BRM were to build the chassis and Velocette the engine. Anyway, the project was stillborn, and it was probably just as well; but similar ideas backed by more enthusiasm than engineering ability continued to exercise various minds for some years, all to no avail. The racing Honda 500 might be an absolute beast to ride, its frame visibly whipping and lozenging and distorting whenever the engine's throttles were wound open,

188

Honda CB750 **(171)**

and giving Hailwood the most difficult rides of his extremely varied and hectic career; but it was scarcely possible to imagine any known British manufacturer coming up with a rival.

The British are always reluctant to see a known firm passing to oblivion; and it was amidst general rejoicing that the old firm of Cotton was briefly reborn in 1968. They produced a couple of 250 c.c. two-stroke machines (one a racer, the other appearing in alternative guises as scrambler or trials iron), but little good was expected to come of it and despite the efforts of the outstanding rider Derek Minter (better known for his exploits in top-class racing), the revival was doomed to failure. In fact, in 1968 it was difficult to resist the conclusion that all expertise in two-strokes was centred in Japan. However, this idea might with some justification be contested by Bultaco in Spain, by Maico in Germany and by cz and Jawa in Czechoslovakia, all of which were prominent and successful in off-road competition where the sole remaining competitive four-stroke was the Swedish Husqvarna. Actually Bultaco made the occasional remarkably rapid road-racer as well, as did their compatriots Montesa; but Japan's Yamahas (by-product of a firm whose greatest contribution to civilization has been some first-class musical instruments) were establishing a virtual stranglehold on the 250 and 350 c.c. racing classes, while Suzuki were equally effective in the 125 class and enjoyed tremendous success in scrambles as well.

Of course, the mainstay of both these motorcycle factories was the road-going

machine, usually of small capacity and often utilitarian specification; but in 1968 Suzuki introduced their new Cobra, a 500 c.c. twin of unusually long wheelbase, surprisingly good handling, and an undeniable turn of speed. Almost as formidable as its perform-ance was its fuel consumption: two-strokes were getting so highly tuned, even in road-going versions, that their thirsts were verging on the ludicrous. The Suzuki gave 47 b.h.p. from its half-litre, but at less than forty miles per gallon its range was necessarily some-what limited.

This did not seem to deter the customers. Their cry was now for more and more power, for better and better acceleration, and they would suffer nothing to get in their way. Whether the machine behaved well at three-figure speeds was of academic interest, for few of them rode that fast. Indeed few of them could, for the riding positions dictated by fashionable high-wide handlebars made the maximum speed of the new generation of superbikes something to be determined not by engine power and gearing but rather by the rider's grip on the handlebars.

Being satisfied of this new demand, BSA-Triumph decided to release a new model that they had had on the stocks for some time, a 750 c.c. three-cylinder machine based on the cylinder dimensions and many moving parts of the 500 c.c. Triumph Speed Twin. The new engine with its four-speed gearbox and diaphragm clutch—and no self-starter—weighed 260 lb. but produced about 60 b.h.p. and was quite happy up to about 8,000 r.p.m. It stood upright in a Triumph frame to be called the Trident, or sloped slightly forward in a BSA frame to be called the Rocket 3, and in either context it provided very strong acceleration with an impressively high maximum speed, being capable of a genuine 120 m.p.h. with the rider prone—always supposing that he could manage such a position and yet maintain control of the big beast through those great unwieldy American-style handlebars. The machine weighed nearly 500 lb. and relied on the smallish drum brakes of the old Bonneville 650 to stop it. They were hardly competent to do so, the front one fading away before completing a high-rate stop from 100 m.p.h. Some compensation was provided by tyres, low-profile trigonal-section Dunlops of exceptional grip and nice predictability which helped the machine to handle a good deal better than its bulk and weight distribution might indicate. Unfortunately the sit-up-and-beg riding position aggravated the rearward-biased weight distribution at high speeds, the rider presenting such a high frontal area as to create a strong moment about the back wheel making the front end light and the steering somewhat vague at three-figure speeds. As we said, the objection was somewhat academic: the customers wanted this superbike for acceleration, not for sustained high speeds.

You could see the sort of customers that BSA and Triumph were after, simply by looking at the garish trim and unconvincing display of chromium exhaust systems. The three cylinders fed two downpipes by the expedient of the centre cylinder having its exhaust downpipe bifurcated to mate with the outer two—and the twin pipes discharged into silencers from each of which issued three tailpipes. It looked absurd.

Nevertheless one had to accept that these were powerful, fast, quite well-behaved and not inordinately thirsty machines. They obviously had tremendous potential for develop-ment into road-burners of real quality, and after a year or so of rather unconvincing experiment they did evolve into production racers of exceptional speed, stamina and apparent controllability.

They certainly needed to, for in 1969 appeared the long-awaited road-going Honda 4. This too was a 750, but it had four cylinders set athwartships as in the racers, and sur-mounted by a single chain-driven overhead camshaft. It had a five-speed gearbox, and

Brands Hatch, 1971, and the start of an international race. Everybody seems to have a Yamaha **(172)**

Honda CB750 front disc brake (173)

of course it had an electric starter. It had a disc brake on its front wheel, a huge 12-inch disc, bigger than any other seen on a motorcycle before or since. Moreover, there was provision on the other leg of the front forks for a matching disc to be mounted; and the drum brake on the rear wheel was larger than that on the front wheel of the BSA-Triumph 750. To be fair, the weight was slightly greater—but only slightly, though the 'bike certainly looked very massive. It belied its looks when on the move, handling with surprising docility and accuracy, for the frame seemed to suffer none of the shortcomings that had characterized earlier Honda heavyweights, while the engine was actually in a very mild state of tune despite its 9:1 compression ratio and 67 b.h.p. output. It marked a departure from earlier Honda practice in having plain steelbacked shell bearings for the big ends and five main bearings of the crankshaft; but the design was characteristically Honda in the extensive use of beautiful die-castings, in the provision of a very full and effective electrical system, and in an abundance of detailed niceties such as the edge-lit dials for the big speedometer and rev-counter, the latter red-lined at 8,500 r.p.m. Maximum speed in neutral conditions with the rider prone corresponded to 8,000 r.p.m. in top gear, equivalent to 125 m.p.h. The sound of the exhaust, restrained in volume but characteristically crisp and high in pitch, was such as to make this or any other speed a rewarding experience rather than a shattering one, but again the riding position contrived to make such speeds well-nigh impossible except for men with short bodies and long strong arms and legs.

Needless to say, it did not take long before the promise implicit in the design was being investigated by sporting riders who reckoned that they had to do little but fit narrow clip-on handlebars and rear-set footrests to turn this into a convincing mount for production machine races. It was mildly successful but not eminently so, until Honda

Yielding at last to necessity, Geoff Duke switches from Norton to Gilera for 1954 **(174)**

set about doing the job properly. When they had finished they had a machine that could run around the Daytona (Florida) Raceway as fast as any and longer than most, while contriving to look surprisingly standard despite most of its castings being in magnesium instead of the standard aluminium alloy, while of course the internals were modified as much as the Daytona regulations would admit.

The annual 200 miles race at Daytona became in the late 1960s the most important race of the year to any manufacturer who took his job seriously enough to set some store by the American market. Success at Daytona was success in American showrooms; it was as simple as that. The rules demanded that the engine of the racer be based on a machine in current quantity production, but most other details were left to the designers' ingenuity or originality. Honda, BSA-Triumph, Suzuki and Yamaha all took the event with tremendous seriousness, Yamaha putting up astonishing performances with engines of only 350 c.c. amidst all the bigger bangers, but never managing quite enough to win, until at last they made it by default in 1972.

Another firm making a determined onslaught on the new American superbike market was Kawasaki, the Japanese aircraft and heavy industry firm, who created something of a furore by following up their lively 250 and 350 two-stroke twins with a three-cylinder 500 that had the reputation of being sudden death on two wheels. It was much lighter than any of the other so-called superbikes, it was as powerful as most of them, giving 60 b.h.p. from its 500 c.c. at no greater cost than could be measured by a really good big fuel flowmeter, and it accelerated so fast that the front wheel could be kept aviated for tremendous distances. The handling rapidly got a bad reputation, for the weight distribution was definitely rearwards, the front forks had very long travel (another feature that was being cultivated to appease a current American fashion for riding off the highway) and the combination of these things with a rather sudden access of power as the throttle opened and the revs soared upwards could make the machine very erratic in a corner. Racing versions, of course, could have these solecisms modified out, and they were always very fast though never really in the picture at Daytona. In minor events in Europe, and rather remarkably in Australia where a standard production Kawasaki 500 was ridden to victory by a girl amateur against strong competition from male stars on racing machinery, so frequently as to cause considerable embarrassment—on occasions such as these the Kawasaki did quite well. On the road it was unbeatable in a straight line. Furthermore, it was nowhere near as expensive as some of the other super-bikes.

Apart from such follies as the big 670-pound Harley-Davidson Electraglide or the powerful NSU-engined Münch Mammut, the highest priced motorcycles had for some years traditionally been the BMW flat twins. These had been plugging along quietly and soberly and not necessarily all that slowly since the early 1950s, undergoing a few changes to frame design in the late 'fifties when they acquired Earles-type front forks and swinging-arm near forks, and occasionally doing quite well at long-distance racing such as the Barcelona twenty-four hours event, not to mention an inspired attack on world records in 1961 when a highly tuned version of the 600 c.c. R69S exceeded 109 m.p.h. for twenty-four hours. Needless to say, this was a good deal faster than the outright maximum speed of the production R69S, which was itself the fastest model in the range that had been introduced in 1956. Of course, BMW had done a fair amount of racing in the intervening years, without notable success in solo events, but with complete domination of the sidecar classes, and the engine of the record breaker undoubtedly leant very heavily on this experience. However, the BMW was, in its production form, at best a luxury

Harley-Davidson KR.TT 750 c.c., here seen in the hands of George Roeder at Meadowdale Raceway, Illinois (175)

sporting tourer, with neither the power nor the gearing nor, indeed, the handling to qualify it as a mount with any pretensions to sporting glamour. In any case, BMW were in the throes of a managerial revolution that was to set them on an entirely new course, establishing them as car manufacturers of no mean order, and for a while there was some doubt as to whether motorcycle production would continue. Eventually the decision was made in favour of continuing with two-wheelers, but with machines of entirely new design; and these appeared late in 1969.

The new engines were still transverse horizontally-opposed twins, still with unit clutch and engine-speed input to the gearbox, still with shaft drive to the rear wheels. Otherwise everything was new, from the long-travel telescopic front forks to the upswept silencers. The engines had been completely redesigned, looking now much more massive but much smoother and cleaner, while concealing within them new plain-bearing crankshafts (instead of the old whippy roller-bearing type) upon which ran conrods taken straight from the six-cylinder BMW 2800 car. Above this huge engine sat a $5\frac{1}{4}$ gallon fuel tank. Within the crankcase castings was a 180 watt alternator. Moreover, the 500 and 600 c.c. versions were augmented by a new 750, for which 57 b.h.p. was claimed—yet the new machine weighed about 20 lb. less than its predecessors, which may have mollified the discovery that its brakes were neither bigger nor better.

This was to be a motorcycle for the connoisseur. It was certainly not one that would satisfy the rider avid for ephemeral sensation, for it still felt like a luxury sporting tourer. It was still a quiet machine, very smooth, one that could be ridden hard and fast without attracting attention to itself—and therein lay much of its appeal, for it was essentially much more practical than some of its supposed rivals. An electric starter confirmed the practicality, clumsy and erratic constant-vacuum carburettors tending to deny it on the 750, but overall it remained what the BMW had long been thought—a machine to buy and keep for travelling long distances in decent comfort and at respectable speeds rather than one to take out and fling about for the sheer fun of it.

Certainly nobody would have been tempted to go out and fling about the BMW's doughtiest big-capacity high-price rival, the V4 Ducati Apollo. This was a big machine indeed, conceived specifically for the American market, its huge air-cooled four-stroke engine supposedly delivering 140 b.h.p. and allowing the Apollo to reach 140 m.p.h. It did not go into production, and by the time that Ducati had come to their senses with more practical if old-fashioned V-twins of 500 and 750 c.c. at the end of 1970, they were in such rocky straits that the Italian Government had to buy them out and thus ensure their future.

In any case there were many people who were now wanting to get their motorcycling fun differently, on machines considerably smaller than these now too-specialized Autobahnstormers. The new cult was trail riding, on machines that the enthusiastic French described as *motos vertes*. Once again the idea was one that Honda may be seen to have started when they put on the American market in the mid-'sixties machines that were ostensibly scramblers but factually sporting roadsters. The name 'street scrambler' caught the imagination of many young American riders, and they took it at its face value to imply that they could ride it not only on the road but also off it—not necessarily in competition but simply for fun. American roads and American society being what they are, the outback was a good place to go motorcycling, and a strong demand was voiced for lightweight, lively, but easily managed, bicycles that were blessed with such qualities of ground clearance, steering, and tractive effort, as would make them competent over the most varied types of going. BSA-Triumph climbed on the bandwagon with alacrity,

196

Dunstall 750 Norton-engined racer, 1970 **(176)**

as did many others. The most telling success was that of the Suzuki Trailcat, a simple pseudo-trials machine with a range-change transmission in which a three-speed gearbox was supplemented by another two-speed gearset, giving one set of ratios for riding on the road and another lower set for riding off it.

When considered as a sport rather than as a recreation, off-highway riding is the speciality of Europeans. The Swedes, the Belgians, the Czechs, the British, all practise it with some assiduity, the British and Belgians having been the leading protagonists in the 1930s when the sport was first developed as a means of combining the rough-riding qualities of sporting trials with the speed and massed-start competitiveness of an out-right race. Nowadays it is nowhere more popular than in France, a country which has seen a tremendous upsurge in the popularity of motorcycling in the latter half of the 1960s, so that the market there may now be considered the most important outside America. The Japanese manufacturers give it a clear priority over all other European countries. Each year the French run more than 300 scrambles, though their word for the sport is 'motocross'. The sport has seen many changes in its machines as the years have gone by, the Early English Perpendicular four-strokes of BSA, Royal Enfield, and

197

Ariel giving way, along with the Belgian Sarolea, FN, and Gillet-Herstal, to the all-conquering two-strokes whose provenance ranges from Japan to Czechoslovakia. The predominant class is for 500 c.c. machines, but there is another classification for 250s, and it is not at all uncommon for the most successful machines to look very much alike in each class and for their engines to be not greatly dissimilar in displacement. For example, there is very little evidence to show whether a championship-winning Suzuki is a 250 or a 370 c.c. machine, other than by taking the engine apart to examine it.

There are, of course, still some four-strokes in competition, notably the tall Swedish Husqvarna. Swedish riders have been prominent in the lists too, with four of them taking eight world championships between 1957 and 1971. They were Nilsonn, Lundin, Tibblin and Aberg, each with two championships to his credit, as had the Englishman Smith in 1964 and 1965 when he was riding BSAs. Only the CZ rider Friedrichs could claim a hat-trick for the years 1966, 1967 and 1968, his machines being of 360, 380 and 420 c.c. respectively, and we may note that despite the permission of a full half-litre, the reigning World Champion Roger de Coster, of Belgium, rode a Suzuki whose engine mustered only 387 c.c. As already observed, it is substantially the same machine as the 250 c.c. Suzuki that took the Belgian Joel Robert to a world championship in the 250 c.c. class in 1970 and 1971 after two preceding victories riding for the CZ company. However, the sport is very much one for individuals, the machines showing very little originality or engineering virtuosity apart from their highly-developed two-stroke engines, and even they cannot be viewed with any great wonder in these days of prodigious power from road-going two-strokes.

Outside Britain the motorcycle seems to be booming and the 1971 Tokyo Show had more than 200 machines on show to prove it. Technically the most interesting was the new 750 c.c. Yamaha 4, a water-cooled transverse two-stroke with fuel injection. This was only a prototype, but the production machines exhibited shortly afterwards in London at a show of racing and sporting motorcycles contained a number of other bright ideas worthy of pursuit. Perhaps the most important thing about the show was that nearly all the significant progress was being made by the small specialist firms. It cannot be that they are any better endowed with reasoning or imaginative brains than the big firms established in the industry; must it not be, then, that they are more closely in touch with what is wanted, as well as being by virtue of their size more flexible in changing their specifications and methods? Most of these little firms are run by people who regularly use the machines they build, who know what is what, and who are not afraid to tell a customer that he is wrong.

By contrast, the big manufacturers (especially, now, certain Japanese ones) are evidently prepared to turn out the most outrageous and impractical nonsense in order to satisfy the imagined needs and ludicrous fancies of an inexperienced clientèle. Wildly powerful and ill-balanced bicycles newly on their stands enforce riding positions that make it impossible to exploit their power with safety. Well-founded cynicism tells us that it is these sops to popular tastelessness which make profits. But the customers are a floating, faithless lot and cannot be relied on to continue to buy these unsuitable models.

All progress, Samuel Butler wrote, *is based upon a universal innate desire on the part of every organism to live beyond its income.* For years, decades even, this has been the defence of the motorcycle industry to accusations that their products were not revealing any progress. Of course, they maintained, they could make better machines; but of course, they insisted, the customers could not or would not pay for them. Today, when the £600 ($1,500) motorcycle is commonplace, their defence becomes invalid. It seems

Moto-Cross Metisse with Rickman-modified BSA engine (177)

that if a motorcycle manufacturer specializes he can charge whatever he likes and the customers will come; and if he does not specialize but is content to churn out unimaginative reproductions of age-old designs, then he can charge what he likes but the customers will stay away.

It does not follow from this that the products of the specialists are particularly progressive. They are faster, they may handle better and brake more surely—the latest Dresda, with a Suzuki Cobra 500 engine in its lightweight frame, provides the most satisfying evidence of this—but unfortunately they are still, beneath the glamour and gimmickry that are evident in most of them, old-fashioned motorcycles. Design has simply not kept pace with progress in other fields. Consider the cars of seventy years ago and compare them with those of today. Consider the trains, the ships, and most of all the aircraft. They have changed, all of them, beyond recognition; but motorcycles? No, there is a more than superficial resemblance between those that led us into the 1970s and those that brought us into the 1900s. Evolution, which grinds small but grinds exceeding slowly, has been painfully and expensively apparent; but of revolutions we have seen almost none. The ancient New Werner, which emerged from the chaos of primitive powered pushbikes when the twentieth century began, still broadly defines the motorcycle as we know it today.

Yet when we lament the ill-balanced engine or curved frame tubes of some ostensibly modern motorcycle, as we are so often able to do, we are not propounding any novelty. As long ago as 1918 there was a London meeting of the Institution of Automobile Engineers at which a great deal of critical attention was given to the current state of motorcycle engineering. It was in the course of this discussion that Mr George Lanchester (who died in 1970 after a long life, in which he enjoyed the sustained respect of most engineers) made the observation quoted at the heading of this chapter.

The study commenced in 1918 by the Institution was pursued through several more meetings continuing into 1923, nine papers being delivered to that learned society. The whole proceedings were eventually bound into a volume with two further papers delivered in the 1925–6 session, including one on the elimination of noise in a motorcycle. Since they embarked on their spate of criticism more than half a century has elapsed, but much of that old criticism still holds good today.

This may seem far-fetched when we compare today's engines with those of 1918, or for that matter those of 1948. Of course, our engines today are more reliable, more powerful and more flexible. Some of them are even more smooth, though there are still dozens of engines that do not even have perfect primary balance and scarcely any in which secondary, rocking, and whirling couples have been eliminated. But we must make a distinction between the motor and the motorcycle, for the developments that have taken place over the years in our engines merely reflect developments that have occurred in parallel in other vehicles, the modern two-stroke's disc valve constituting the only major exception to the rule. The trouble is that people understand engines a great deal better than they understand frames and steering; they are naïve enough to get more satisfaction out of blasting their way to the front of any group of vehicles on the road than from, say, being able to ride the machine to a standstill with the hands off the steering, as could be done on a 1925 Ner-A-Car. Give the customer another 250 c.c., another cylinder, another 10 or 20 b.h.p., and he is content even if the beast ties its frame into knots. Too much motor and not enough cycle, that is the trouble.

What about that no-man's-land that comes between the motor and the cycle? The transmission, I mean: since about 1930 it has changed less than anything else except the shape of the wheels. Is this not extraordinary? Can it be right that what was considered an imperfect system even forty years ago should not be capable of improvement? It is one of the paradoxes of motor transport that vehicles whose motion must be controllable from standstill up to an increasingly high maximum speed should be powered by engines which in their delivery of power and torque and in their range of controllable operating speeds are fundamentally ill-suited to the task: in relieving the keenness of this paradox the stepped-ratio gearbox transmission merely alleviates the symptoms without curing the disease. Why is there not a modern motorcycle with hydrokinetic transmission? A simple three-element torque convertor would be suited better than the Heath Robinson contraptions that must by now be a wasting inheritance. Another few years and it may be time for hydrostatic transmission, which will finally get rid of the question of shaft drive's superiority to chain, a question that should never have arisen.

Even the arrangement of clutch and gearbox on our motorcycles is ancient and suspect, as it was in 1918. Then, let us consider the steering. The majority of motorcycles today have telescopic front forks; those that do not rely on some system of leading or trailing links, no version of which gives fully satisfactory steering geometry. The telescopic fork should do this, but commonly does not, being a weak structure ill-suited to the job. In the first place the front wheel spindle is never sufficiently substantial nor adequately clenched in the sliders to ensure the transverse stiffness and freedom from

One of the chair-racing brothers Hanks at Druids Hill Bend, Brands Hatch, in the 1971 Hutchinson 100 **(178)**

lozenging that the forks themselves are unable to provide. If the spindle cannot be better proportioned and located, then the sliders must be firmly joined so that they cannot move other than in perfect unison. To be on the safe side they should not operate severally on separate springs in each fork leg but jointly on a central suspension unit. Furthermore, they should be relieved of all non-axial loads which can cause the sliding surfaces to bind and thus impair suspension movement. This cannot be done, so the sliders ought to embody linear ball-bearings running on the fork stanchions. Even so, the sliders and stanchions are subjected to bending loads which cannot be good for them or for the steering.

What a sorry substitute it all is for good substantial hub-centre steering, not the little ineffectual kingpins such as might have sufficed for the low-powered Ner-A-Car, but big accurate ones such as might fill a modern brake drum. There is room there, for drum brakes should now be a thing of the past on anything other than ultra-lightweights. At long last the disc brake is catching on, and so is hydraulic actuation; but we should have had these things ten years ago.

There is even less excuse for bad frame design, for the principles are widely known, reasonably well understood, and can, if properly interpreted, admit worthwhile economies in manufacture. Instead, what we get are amorphous blacksmithing jobs, bits of bent tubing beefed up until they are too heavy to break. Back in 1918 they were complaining because machines were gradually getting heavier, until a 500 c.c. roadster which had formerly weighed 190 lb. now weighed 260 lb. You would be lucky to find one weighing less than 400 lb. now, and no wonder! The reasons are exactly the same as those identified by Mr D. S. Heather at the opening session of that 1918 meeting: *The method adopted to obtain reliability in the past has frequently been to pile on metal at the faulty place until breakages no longer occurred, when by reasonable design reliability might have been obtained without any increase of weight. The author hopes then that future designs will provide motorcycles which are cleaner, more comfortable, more reliable, and more durable, and which weigh less than those of current types.*

Some hopes! Nobody, it seems, is interested in reasonable design. Take the frame of any current motorcycle on the market that is built of steel tubing. *No engineer can claim that this is a properly designed structure in which the metal is so disposed as to resist in the most efficient manner possible the stresses imposed upon it. As a matter of fact, it is obviously nothing but an adaptation of an ordinary pedal cycle diamond frame. It breaks every rule which governs the design of steel structures and is actually only held in shape by the strength of lugs or tube junctions which should not be called upon to prevent distortion.* This is 1918 comment again, but it is still substantially true. There is seldom any proper means of dealing with engine and gearbox torque reactions, which tend in consequence to produce miserable distortion of the frame, which is only resisted by the stiffness of the tubes as beams and the stiffness of the lugs, if any, though these are mercifully becoming rare.

Nor are torque reactions the only ones to affect the frame: lateral bending loads applied by the asymmetric transmission, together with other miscellaneous ones fed in through the suspension and all the various loads, fixed and otherwise, that the frame is supposed to be able to bear, play havoc with its dimensional integrity, for today's frames still have very little torsional stiffness or lateral rigidity. The frames, therefore, have to be made exceedingly heavy for the duties they have to bear, and are even then far from satisfactory when worked really hard. Indeed the process of stiffening by adding extra metal can accelerate failure.

There is really no excuse for this at all. No self-respecting designer should be prepared

Royal Enfield 750 c.c. Interceptor Road Scrambler (Export to U.S.A. only) **(179)**

to produce a frame incorporating tubes that are bent or that are subjected to bending loads. All the bends and curlicues of a BSA frame, the now classical curvature of a Norton Featherbed, or even the varying ovality of tube sections in a BMW, is all so much eye-wash. The tubes should be dead straight, and arranged so as to be loaded only in tension or compression, in an arrangement fully triangulated in all planes to ensure structural stability under all anticipated loads. In the whole history of the motorcycle there have been very few such frames, very few indeed. The last must have been the racing Guzzi of 1957, a machine that was remarkably modern in many ways despite its one-lung engine. The splendid frame design usually went unnoticed, for in those days racing motorcycles were streamlined or faired, and Guzzi made the most of a full-scale wind tunnel to ensure wind-cheating ability superior to that of practically all competitors.

Here is another thing that motorcycle designers and manufacturers just do not seem to care about. The drag coefficient of a solo motorcycle is simply appalling, which explains why the things so often run out of acceleration at high speed and why their fuel consumption is so high. Many motorcycles are uncomfortable to ride because there is no room or no provision for adopting a riding position that gives some relief from the gymnastics of staying in control despite wind pressure. In too many cases maximum speed is determined by the strength of the rider's fingers, on which he has to rely to keep hold of the handlebars and thereby resist being blown off the back of the saddle. We

New Year's Day 1972. That is rising racing star Barry Sheene on the Suzuki-engined Difazio. The main feature is Joe Difazio's hub-centre steering (180)

probably have the reverent elders who govern our sport to thank for this; back in the 1950s, finding that they did not adequately understand streamlining—and finding that the streamlining then current sometimes caused handling problems, though these were invariably due to the need to comply with regulations that the Sporting Governors had confected in advance—they then forbade full streamlining altogether. Now the current state of motorcycling, and indeed the state during the past dozen years, has seen to it that if racers do not employ full fairings the roadsters will not either, since we insist on road machines looking like racers. Too often they only succeed in making the things look like superannuated vintage 'bikes—but this is understandable because nearly all today's machines *are* vintage 'bikes.

There would be many benefits from efficient fairings. Not only would the speed, acceleration and economy be materially improved; not only could the problems of establishing a decent riding position be resolved by getting out of the draught; but also a whole host of revisions could be made to accepted notions of motorcycle structure, to the benefit of all concerned. The fairing need not be an appendage but could be a basic structural member, a stressed-skin hull continuous with the rest of the frame and, perhaps, carrying on its inner surface supporting anchorages and location points for the front suspension, which could thus be kept close to the wheel to which it belongs. Internal aerodynamics would have to be studied as carefully as external ones, with properly ducted air flow to the engine, the (disc) brakes, the (exposed and properly designed) dampers which would replace our present haphazard use of unsuitable engine oil inside unfathomable forks, and so on. The wheels could be made of one of the light alloys such as magnesium Elektron C, or glass- or carbon-reinforced plastics. At any rate, we could get rid of the old and feeble wire wheel.

We could do all these things. But it seems unlikely that we ever shall. There have been one or two brave attempts at these various advances, though no concerted attempt at all of them. Instead it seems that all the attention of designers will be directed by marketing experts at the development of bigger, more powerful, and thirstier engines, while a grudging recognition of the inevitability of disc brakes promises to be the only attention that the cycle will enjoy. The latest three-cylinder 750 c.c. two-strokes from Japan muster more than 70 b.h.p. and ought to be powerful enough for most purposes: yet they are undergeared for the sake of acceleration, and their fuel consumption is so high that on some European motorways they cannot get from one refuelling area to the next.

The marketing men, it seems, have found a new way of getting rich quickly without too much thought for the morrow. Design is not progressing, it is stagnant; and the probable consequences are a depressing subject for speculation. For all their petty changes, motorcycles today are very much as they have always been—but the world in which they find themselves is changing, and, therefore, their relationship to it must alter correspondingly. We have seen how, in the past, the motorcycle progressed from being an engineering experiment to a tool of travel for the lower ranks of society, in the 1950s to degenerate into a means whereby the socially protestant might make themselves obnoxious, and in the 1960s to grow into a therapeutic device with which the fairly well-to-do might rediscover all the joys and painful truths of genuine recreation. In the 1970s the still fundamentally unchanged motorcycle threatens to become the briefly entertained and costly plaything of a spoiled and fashion-bound class of sensation seekers. *Plus c'est la même chose, plus ça change.*

Acknowledgments

Thanks and acknowledgments are due to the following for the use of copyright illustrations:

The Science Museum, London, Plates numbers 1, 3, 6, 7, 11, 25, 28, 32, 36, 75, 82, 102
Deutsches Zweirad-Museum, Neckarsulm, W. Germany, 2, 4
The Montagu Motor Museum, Beaulieu, England, 35, 42, 46–9, 51, 60, 62–3, 65, 68, 70, 77–9, 90, 92, 95–101, 103, 107–10, 114–15, 121–2, 124–7, 129–30, 132, 135–42, 144, 153–6, 158
Harley-Davidson Motor Co, Milwaukee, USA, 39–41, 151, 159, 175
Radio Times Hulton Picture Library, 43–5, 50, 52, 55, 66, 67, 73, 87, 112, 148, 152
BMW, W. Germany, 123, 128, 134, 143, 145–6, 161–2
Press Association, London, 149, 157, 174
Black Star, London, 160
Brian Holder, 163
The Motor Cycle, Iliffe Publications Ltd, London, 166, 168, 170

The authors' thanks are also due for assistance to Alan Baker, Cyril Ayton and Cyril Quantrill.

Index

ABC, 41, 43–4, 73–4, 82, 84, 118
Aberg, 198
Ace, 78, 122
Acme, 104
Aermacchi, 174
Agostini, D., 174
Agostini, G., 174, 188
Agusta, MV, 166, 168, 173, 184, 188
AJS, 82, 88, 92, 94–6, 104, 110, 132, 145–6, 153, 156–7, 161, 180
All British Engineering Co, 43
AMAC, 86
Amal Carburettors, 86, 152
AMC, 161, 180
Amm, R., 173
Anderson, F., 166, 173
Anderson, H., 188
Anzani, 120
Ardie, 142, 156
Armstrong, R., 173
Ariel, 112, 121, 122, 152, 158, 161, 174, 180
Aspi, 152
Associated Motorcycles, 180
Atlas, 178, 180
Avon tyres, 170, 173
Azzariti, 127

Barr and Stroud, 67
Barry, 38
Beardmore Precision, 82
Belgian GP (see Racing)
Bell, A., 156–7
Benelli, 145–6
Bennett, A., 88, 95, 104, 129
Bianchi, 104, 168
Binks, 38
Blackburn, 82
BMW, 38, 55, 73, 84, 118, 129, 138, 140, 142, 145–7, 153, 156, 166, 173–4, 179, 194, 196, 203
Bonnicksen, 40
Bosch, 29, 56
Bosch, R., 29, 40
Boudeville magneto, 29
Bradshaw, G., 43, 73–4
BRM, 188
Brockhouse, 161
Brooklands (see Racing)
Brough, G., 86, 88, 95, 122, 144
Brough Superior, 82, 86, 88, 92, 95–6, 107–8, 117, 120, 122, 124, 126, 129, 138, 140, 149, 156
Brough, W., 86
Brown & Barlow, 86
BSA, 88, 120, 152, 161, 174, 178–9, 181, 184, 191–2, 194, 196–8, 203
Bucquet, 32
Bultaco, 170, 180, 189
Butler, E., 11–13, 29

Cann, M., 157
Castle forks, 92, 107
Chater Lea, 41, 96, 104
Circuit of Cremona (see Racing)
Clark, R. H., 107
Cleveland, 122
Coleman, 173
Collier, C., 46, 51, 56

Collier, H., 46, 51
Condor, 151
Copeland, 10
Cotton, 104, 135, 189
Coventry Motor Co, 26
Coventry Victor, 92, 141
Cox-Atmos, 117
Craig, J., 95
Cucciolo, 153
CZ, 179, 198

Daimler, 11–12, 36
Daimler, G., 11
Dale, D., 173
Darracq, 13
Davies, H., 96
Daytona (see Racing)
Dax, 141
de Coster, R., 198
de Dion Bouton, 28, 30, 32, 43
de Dion, Count A., 10, 14
de Rochas, 11
Dresda, 199
Dixon, F., 92
DKW, 107, 114, 129, 134, 137–8, 142, 144–6, 170, 178
Dobson, C., 146
Douglas, 38, 44, 56, 73, 82, 94, 108, 110, 118, 148–52, 161, 174
Doughty, 154
Dragonfly, 38
Ducati, 166, 168, 174, 180
Duke, G., 162, 173, 196
Dunelt engine, 78
Dunlop, J. B., 28
Dunlop tyres, 170
Dunstall, P., 184
Dutch TT (see Racing)

Earles fork, 194
EMC, 154
Enfield, 30, 43
Erlich, 154
Excelsior, 7, 35, 144–6
Eysink, 144, 157

Fafnir, 41
Fernihough, E., 138
FN, 38, 73–4, 122, 141
Fowler, R., 46
Francis Barnett, 94, 180
French GP (see Racing)
Friedrichs, 198
Frith, F., 137, 144, 157, 161–2

Gareli, 104
German GP (see Racing)
Ghersi, 103–4
Giannini, 145
Gibson, 26
Gilera, 127, 142, 145, 152, 156–7, 166, 168, 171
Gillet-Herstal, 198
Gnome et Rhone, 84, 141
Graham, L., 157, 166, 173
Graham, S., 188
Griffon, 84

Grimeca brakes, 183
Guthrie, J., 132–4
Guzzi, 103–4, 122, 134–5, 137–8, 144–6, 152, 154, 156–8, 162, 166, 168, 173, 182–3, 203

Haas, W., 166, 173
Haden, 182
Hailwood, M., 173, 188–9
Handley, W., 104, 129
Harley-Davidson, 36, 65, 73, 92, 120, 140, 156, 158, 174, 178, 194
Heath, P., 158
Hedstrom, O., 36
Hele, D., 184
Hendee, G., 36
Henderson, 78, 122
Henne, E., 138
Hildebrand, 13–14
Hildebrand and Wolfmuller, 14, 29, 43
Hocking, G., 173
Holden. H. C., 14
Honda, 94, 168, 170, 176, 179–80, 182, 184, 188, 192, 194, 196
HRD, 96, 117
Humber, 26
Husqvarna, 134, 142, 189, 198

Imola, 173
Imperian, 129
Inchley, P., 188
Indian, 7, 36, 40–1, 46, 65, 73, 78, 92, 107, 120, 135, 140, 156, 174
Irving, 149
Isle of Man TT (see Racing)
Ivy, W., 92, 188

James, 180
JAP, 44, 46, 73, 82, 86, 88, 94, 96, 108, 120
Jawa, 134, 179, 189
Jowett, 43, 54
Junak, 179

Kaaden, W., 179
Kavanagh, K., 173
Kawasaki, 194
Kingsbury, 84
Kluge, 146
Knight, 12
Kreidler, 170

Lagonda, 44
Lanchester, G., 200
Laverda, 182–3
Lawrence, T. E., 129
Lea Francis, 156
Lenoir, E., 10
Le Vack, H., 92, 94, 96
Lockett, 157
Lockheed brakes, 184
Lorenzetti, 157, 174
Lundin, 198
Lyons, E., 151, 154
Lyster, C., 184

Mabeco, 107
M A G, 88
Maico, 189
Manx G P (*see* Racing)
Marchant, D., 153
Martin, H., 35
Martin & Handasyde, 88
Martinsyde, 88, 92
Masetti, 174
Masserini, 156–7
Matchless, 44, 56, 82, 88, 104, 118,
    122, 124, 156, 161, 180
Maybach, W., 11
McIntyre, R., 168, 170, 173
Meek, 10
Meier, G., 146
Mellors, F., 145–6
Michel, 10
Milani, 174
Millet, 13
Minerva, 30, 36
Minter, D., 189
Montesa, 189
Montgomery, 96
Moore, 30
Morgan, 86
Morini, 157
Motosacoche, 124, 144, 153, 156
Münch Mammut, 194
M V Agusta (*see* Agusta)
M Z, 170, 178–9

Ner-A-Car, 94, 200, 202
Neracher, 94
Neokarsulm, 30
New Imperial, 92, 94, 120
Nilsom, 198
Nimbus, 127, 142
Norton, 46, 51, 92, 95, 104, 110, 129,
    132, 134–5, 137, 140, 144–6, 152,
    156–7, 161–2, 164, 166, 168, 173–4,
    179–81, 184, 203
N S U, 30, 36, 41, 129, 142, 146, 156,
    166, 168, 174
Nurbügring, 173
Nuvolari, T., 95, 132

O E C, 117
O K-Blackburn, 129
O S A, 179
Otto, Dr N., 10–11

P & M, 30, 43, 56, 120, 122
Pagani, N., 152
Panther, 30, 154
Parilla, 152
Parkyns, Sir T., 10
Patria, 104
Peugeot, 36, 46, 82, 84
Phelon, J., 30
Philipp, F., 46
Phillis, T., 173

Poppe, E., 150
Potts, J., 168
Prestwich, J. A., 36, 67, 86, 110
Püch, 36, 114, 142

Quadrant, 30, 44, 84

Racing:
    Belgian G P, 95, 129
    Brooklands, 44, 46, 74, 92
    Brooklands 22 miles, 95
    Brooklands 500 miles, 92
    Circuit of Cremona, 95
    Clubman's T T, 158
    Daytona, 194
    Dutch T T, 156
    French G P, 88, 95, 129
    German G P, 132
    International 6-days Trial, 179
    Land's End to John o' Groat's, 46
    Manx G P, 152, 154, 162
    1,000 Miles Trial, 46
    Paris–Madrid race, 44
    Spanish 12-hour race, 95
    Swiss G P, 158
    T T, 41, 44, 46, 56, 82, 94–6, 103,
        127, 134, 137, 144–6, 153–4, 156,
        162, 166, 168, 184, 188
    Ulster G P, 95, 157
Raleigh, 82
Ratier, 179
Reed, P., 188
Redman, 173
Redrup, 65, 122
Regent, 82
Rex Acme, 104, 129, 156
Reynolds, 84
Ricardo, H., 67, 92
Robert, J., 198
Rickman brothers, 184
Rondine, 127, 142, 145
Roots, 12
Roper, 10
Royal Enfield, 161, 174, 181, 197
Rosemeyer, B., 132
Rover, 94
Rudge, 41, 44, 56, 104, 132, 146

Sarolea, 141, 198
Schnuerle, Dr, 114, 129
Schütoff, 107
Scott, 41, 43, 56, 66, 88, 94, 96, 114,
    141, 158
Scott, A., 30, 43, 51, 54, 56, 88
Serpollet, L., 10
Shaw, 26
Sheard, T., 94
Sheffield-Simplex, 94
Sheldon, J., 74
S H L, 179
Simms, F., 29
Simpson, J., 104, 132

Simson, 178
Sleischer, 138
Smith, 198
Sopwith, 74
Spanish 12-hour race (*see* Racing)
Sperber, 178
Standard, 142
Sublime, 153
Sun, 82
Sunbeam, 73, 88, 146, 148, 150–1,
    174
Surtees, J., 132, 173
Suzuki, 176, 179, 188–9, 191, 194,
    197–9
Swiss G P (*see* Racing)

Temple, 117
Tenni, O., 134, 144, 157–8
Thomas, 36
Tiblin, 198
Tourist Trophy race (*see* Racing)
Triton, 180
Triumph, 30, 46, 56, 67, 92, 118,
    121–2, 151–2, 154, 161–2, 174,
    179–82, 184, 191–2, 194, 196
Trojan, 114
T T (*see* Racing)
Turner, 121
Tyrell-Smith, 146

Ubbiali, 174
Ulster G P (*see* Racing)
Union, 78, 82
Universal, 153

Varzi, A., 158
Velocette, 104, 110, 118, 129, 137,
    145–6, 154, 157–8, 161–2, 181, 188
Vespa, 153, 161
Victoria, 114, 142, 156
Villiers, 66, 78, 82, 95, 114, 117, 141,
    180, 188
Vincent, 137, 140, 148–50, 154, 158,
    174
Vindec, 46

Ward, D., 180
Werner, 30–2, 35, 43, 199
West, J., 146
White & Poppe, 86, 150
Williams, D., 82
Wolfmuller, A., 14
Wood, T., 56
Woods, S., 104, 134–5, 144, 146
Wooler, 82, 96, 158

Yamaha, 176, 179–80, 189, 194, 198

Zenith, 154
Zündapp, 114, 129, 142, 156